# ICFA Continuing Education
# **Behavioral Finance and Decision Theory in Investment Management**

Proceedings of the AIMR seminar *Improving the Investment Decision-Making Process: Behavioral Finance and Decision Theory*

April 4, 1995
Marina del Rey, California

Horace W. Brock
Werner F.M. De Bondt
David N. Dreman
Russell J. Fuller, CFA
Richard S. Pzena
Leslie Shaw
Meir Statman
Amos Tversky
Arnold S. Wood, *Moderator*

Edited by Arnold S. Wood

To obtain an AIMR Publications Catalog or to order additional copies of this publication, turn to page 65 or contact:

AIMR
P.O. Box 3668
Charlottesville, VA 22903
U.S.A.
Telephone: (804) 980-3668
Fax: (804) 980-9755
E-mail: info@aimr.com
World Wide Web site: http://www.aimr.com/aimr.html

*The Association for Investment Management and Research comprises the Institute of Chartered Financial Analysts and the Financial Analysts Federation.*



*ICFA Continuing Education* is published eight times a year by the Association for Investment Management and Research, P.O. Box 3668, Charlottesville, Virginia 22903. This publication is designed to provide accurate and authoritative information in regard to the subject matter covered. It is sold with the understanding that the publisher is not engaged in rendering legal, accounting, or other professional service. If legal advice or other expert assistance is required, the services of a competent professional should be sought. Application to mail at second class postage rates is pending at Charlottesville, Virginia, and additional mailing offices.

Copies are mailed as a benefit of membership to CFA® charterholders. Subscriptions also are available at $100 for one year. Address all circulation communications to ICFA Continuing Education, P.O. Box 3668, Charlottesville, Virginia 22903; (804) 980-3668; FAX (804) 980-9755. For change of address, send mailing label and new address six weeks in advance.

Postmaster: Send address changes to the Association for Investment Management and Research, P.O. Box 3668, Charlottesville, Virginia 22903.

ISBN 1-879087-57-X

Printed in the United States of America

December 1995

# Contents

Foreword . . . v

Biographies of Speakers . . . vi

Behavioral Finance and Decision Theory in Investment Management: An Overview . . . 1
Arnold S. Wood

The Psychology of Decision Making . . . 2
Amos Tversky

Investor Psychology and the Dynamics of Security Prices . . . 7
Werner F.M. De Bondt

Behavioral Finance versus Standard Finance . . . 14
Meir Statman

The Principal–Agent Relationship and Investment Decision Making . . . 23
Leslie Shaw

Behavioral Biases and Alphas . . . 31
Russell J. Fuller, CFA

Behavioral Biases and Investment Research . . . 36
Richard S. Pzena

Exploiting Behavioral Finance: Portfolio Strategy and Construction . . . 42
David N. Dreman

The Future of Behavioral Finance: A Synthesis of Disciplines . . . 52
Horace "Woody" Brock

Bibliography . . . 58

Self-Evaluation Examination
Questions . . . 61
Answers . . . 62

Selected Publications . . . 63

Order Form . . . 65

## ICFA Board of Trustees, 1995–96



## AIMR Council on Education and Research, 1995–96



## AIMR Senior Education Staff

# Foreword

AIMR is extremely pleased to bring you this proceedings of the first conference we have held that focused on the application of decision theory and behavioral studies to financial and market issues. The rising interest in these approaches has two clear purposes: to find an explanation for the anomalies that continue to baffle the investment profession and to deal with the disappointing performance of active investment management. Insights into these puzzles can help money managers change their thinking and behavior to improve their judgments, their decisions, their performance, and their service to clients.

The presentations in this proceedings offer such insights—from the world of academics and the world of practice. Major investigators of decision theory and behavioral finance analyze and contrast the world view of rational economic models and efficient markets with the human factors that influence the markets—how people act on information and when, the normal human tendencies that create biases, cognitive illusions that affect decision making, and the principal–agent relationship. The importance of wedding behavioral insights to our traditional economic approaches is stated concisely in the following quotation from economist John Maurice Clark: "The economist may attempt to ignore psychology, but it is sheer impossibility for him to ignore human nature."

We hope you will learn from and enjoy this compendium of thoughts on behavioral finance and decision theory in investment management. We call your attention also to the extensive bibliography on decision theory and behavioral finance that follows the presentations in this proceedings. We wish to thank Arnold S. Wood of Martingale Asset Management for serving as the moderator of the seminar and for his astute overview. We also extend our thanks to the speakers for their participation and help with preparing this publication: Horace W. Brock, Strategic Economic Decisions; Werner F.M. De Bondt, University of Wisconsin–Madison; David N. Dreman, Dreman Value Management; Russell J. Fuller, CFA, RJF Asset Management; Richard S. Pzena, Sanford C. Bernstein & Company; Leslie Shaw, Leslie Shaw & Associates; Meir Statman, Santa Clara University; Amos Tversky, Stanford University.

Katrina F. Sherrerd, CFA
Senior Vice President
Education

# Biographies of Speakers

**Horace W. Brock** is founder and president of Strategic Economic Decisions, which he established to apply the new "economics of uncertainty" to a global fixed-income strategy and to asset allocation. Before founding the company, he was a senior member of Stanford Research Institute's International Management and Economics Group. Dr. Brock's commentaries on the world economy have appeared in the *New York Times* and the *International Herald Tribune*. He holds degrees from Harvard and Princeton and has taught at both universities.

**Werner F.M. De Bondt** is Frank Graner Professor of Investment Management at the University of Wisconsin–Madison. As one of the founders of behavioral finance, he uses psychology to interpret financial decision-making phenomena. Dr. De Bondt holds a Ph.D. from Cornell University.

**David N. Dreman** is founder and chairman of Dreman Value Management and director of the company's money management and investment research efforts. Prior to founding the firm, he was director of New York Research for Rauscher Pierce Refsnes, senior investment officer with J&W Seligman, and senior editor with Value Line Publishing. Mr. Dreman is the author of three books about low-P/E investment strategies and is a regular columnist for *Forbes* magazine. He holds a bachelor's degree in commerce from the University of Manitoba.

**Russell J. Fuller, CFA,** is president of RJF Asset Management. Previously, he was vice president and manager of strategy development at Concord Capital Management, security analyst for First Mid-America, general partner and portfolio manager for Capital Investment Group, and vice president and director of research for Connors Investor Services. Dr. Fuller has also served as professor and department chair of finance at Washington State University. He is the author of numerous articles in leading academic and professional journals and co-author of *Modern Investments and Security Analysis*. Dr. Fuller serves on the editorial board of *The Journal of Portfolio Management* and the advisory board of the *Financial Analysts Journal*. He holds a B.A., M.B.A., and Ph.D. from the University of Nebraska.

**Richard S. Pzena** is director of U.S. equity investments and chair of the Research Review Group at Sanford C. Bernstein & Company. Before joining Bernstein, he spent six years with the Amoco Corporation. Mr. Pzena holds a B.S. and an M.B.A. from the Wharton School of the University of Pennsylvania.

**Leslie Shaw** is founder and president of Leslie Shaw & Associates, which provides consulting services on judgment performance to financial firms. She is also an adjunct lecturer in business policy at the University of Chicago's Graduate School of Business for the 1995–96 academic year. Dr. Shaw holds an M.B.A. and a Ph.D. in psychology from the University of Chicago.

**Meir Statman** is professor of finance at the Leavey School of Business of Santa Clara University. For his research on financial decision making, he has received a Batterymarch Financial Management fellowship and research grants from the National Science Foundation and the Research Foundation of the Institute of Chartered Financial Analysts. He is a member of the advisory board of *The Journal of Portfolio Management* and associate editor of the *Internal Review of Financial Analysis*. Dr. Statman holds a B.A. and an M.B.A. from the Hebrew University of Jerusalem and a Ph.D. from Columbia University.

**Amos Tversky** is Davis-Brack Professor of Behavioral Science at Stanford University. Previously, he taught at the Hebrew University in Jerusalem. Dr. Tversky has received the Distinguished Scientific Contribution Award of the American Psychological Association and the MacArthur Prize. He is a member of the National Academy of Sciences and the American Academy of Arts and Sciences. Dr. Tversky holds a B.A. from the Hebrew University in Jerusalem and a Ph.D. from the University of Michigan.

**Arnold S. Wood** is president and CEO of Martingale Asset Management. Before founding Martingale, he was a trustee and senior vice president of Batterymarch Financial Management, where he served as a global investment strategist and portfolio manager. Mr. Wood is a member of the AIMR Board of Governors, a founding member and former president of the International Society of Financial Analysts, former chair of the Financial Analysts Federation, and former president of the Society of Quantitative Analysts. He is the author of several articles that focus on investing and behavioral finance. Mr. Wood is a graduate of Trinity College and attended the Amos Tuck School at Dartmouth.

# Behavioral Finance and Decision Theory in Investment Management: An Overview

Arnold S. Wood
*President and CEO*
*Martingale Asset Management*

Evidence is prolific that money managers rarely live up to expectations. In the search for reasons, academics and practitioners alike are turning to behavioral finance for clues. This new science has old roots. It is the study of us. That 1950s comic-strip character Pogo hit the mark when he said, "We have met the enemy, and he is us." After all, we are human, and we are not always rational in the way equilibrium models would like us to be. Rather, we play games that indulge our self-interest.

John von Neumann, co-author of *The Theory of Games and Human Behavior* (1944), was once asked about chess as a game. He replied,

> Chess is a well-defined form of computation. You may not be able to work out the answers, but in theory there must be a solution, a right procedure in any position. Now, real games are not like that at all. Real life is not like that. Real life consists of bluffing, of little tactics of deception, of asking yourself what is it the other man thinks I meant to do. That, in my mind, is what games are all about.

Financial markets are a real game. They are the arena of fear and greed. Our apprehensions and aspirations are acted out every day in the marketplace. Prices tell the story of von Neumann's sense of the "real game." So, perhaps prices are not always rational and efficiency may be a textbook hoax. For the sake of active managers, let's hope so.

AIMR demonstrated courage in sponsoring the seminar from which this proceedings springs. The seminar questioned how and why we think the way we do and suggested ways to rethink investment problems so that the same old nasty biases would not repeat themselves. People tend to repeat the same errors in judgment day in and day out, and not only do they do it with predictability, they do it with confidence.

For those who are looking for answers to the following questions and many more related to decision theory and behavioral finance, reading this proceedings will provide new and practical insights:

- How do you organize an investment research effort to squeeze out harmful analyst biases?
- How do you exploit the fact that earnings estimates miss reported earnings by as much as 50 percent across the board?
- How can you use the framing of gains and losses (prospect theory) to improve your understanding of alternatives?
- How do you resist the lure of positive company attributes that often draws investors into overvalued stocks?
- Are people really as irrational as current findings of behavioral finance would lead us to believe, or is there an alternative explanation, another paradigm for market behavior?

In a fast-paced business whose objective is to capture higher future asset values, decisions are naturally fraught with difficult-to-recognize heuristics. These judgmental biases are discussed throughout the following presentations, through the eyes of both academic researchers and experienced practitioners. The material is intuitively appealing and anecdotally invigorating. One consistent theme throughout is the force relationships exert on decisions. We operate in a world of the hired (the "agent") and the boss or client (the "principal"). How we deal with and react to one another dictates decision making that pushes the laws of optimality in the classical sense to the background. Behavioral finance and decision theory contain much to be learned. Perhaps, just perhaps, those tired of "the loser's game" will find the decision-making path to "the winner's game."

Finally, as true winner Yogi Berra was once overheard saying, "If you don't know where you're going, you better watch out, 'cause you may not get there." This road map to better decision making will help—a lot.

# The Psychology of Decision Making

Amos Tversky
*Davis-Brack Professor of Behavioral Sciences*
*Stanford University*

Three areas of "cognitive illusion" that violate basic assumptions of the classical economic model of decision making are risk attitudes, mental accounting, and overconfidence. Their existence indicates that the rational economic model is incomplete in a systematic way. The three phenomena also provide clues to many market anomalies and investor phenomena, and understanding these biases may suggest ways to exploit them in the market.

Financial markets are influenced by many complex factors, including economic processes, institutional and political constraints, the flow and dissemination of information, and last but not least, people's reactions to and perceptions of risk. Studies of judgment and decision making indicate that people do not always behave in accord with the classical rational model of economic decision making. The classical analysis assumes that people are perfectly consistent, satisfy criteria of coherence, and have unlimited computational power. The evidence, however, shows that human rationality is bounded by both emotional and cognitive factors.

This presentation addresses some basic elements of the psychology of risk. It does not attempt to provide a comprehensive theory of investor psychology; instead, it reviews and illustrates a few salient findings. Specifically, the discussion focuses on three phenomena—risk attitudes, mental accounting, and overconfidence—that violate basic assumptions of the classical economic model of decision making. These phenomena are often referred to as cognitive illusions because, like visual illusions, they relate to perceptions that often remain compelling and tempting even when people realize they are illusory or fallacious.

## Risk Attitudes

One of the fundamental assumptions of the economic analysis of risk that is built into portfolio theory is the assumption of risk aversion. Analysts assume that, holding expected value constant, people would rather have a certain return than an uncertain return, and that people need to be compensated for bearing risk. Although risk aversion is quite common, it fails in some situations.

Consider the following problem. You have a choice between a sure $85,000 or a risky prospect that offers an 85 percent chance to receive $100,000 and a 15 percent chance to receive nothing. Both prospects have the same expected actuarial value: If you play them over and over again, you will receive on average the same amount. The great majority of people, however, would rather receive $85,000 for sure than take the chance of receiving nothing. This preference illustrates the notion of risk aversion.

Now consider the mirror-image problem. In this case, you face a sure loss of $85,000 or an 85 percent chance of losing $100,000 and a 15 percent chance of losing nothing. The great majority of people would rather take an 85 percent chance of losing $100,000 with a 15 percent chance of losing nothing than a sure loss of $85,000. This preference exhibits risk seeking rather than risk aversion. Thus, risk aversion is not always valid, especially in the domain of losses, where risk seeking is frequently observed.

Because risk aversion does not hold in all cases, a different model from the classical model is called for. **Figure 1** presents a hypothetical value function that captures observed human responses to gains and losses. This S-shaped function has three features that distinguish it from the concave utility function of classical economic analysis. First, it is defined in terms of gains and losses rather than in terms of asset position, or wealth. This approach reflects the observation that people think of outcomes in terms of gains and losses relative to some reference point, such as the status quo, rather than in terms of a final asset position. Because people cannot lose what they do

**Figure 1. A Hypothetical Value Function**

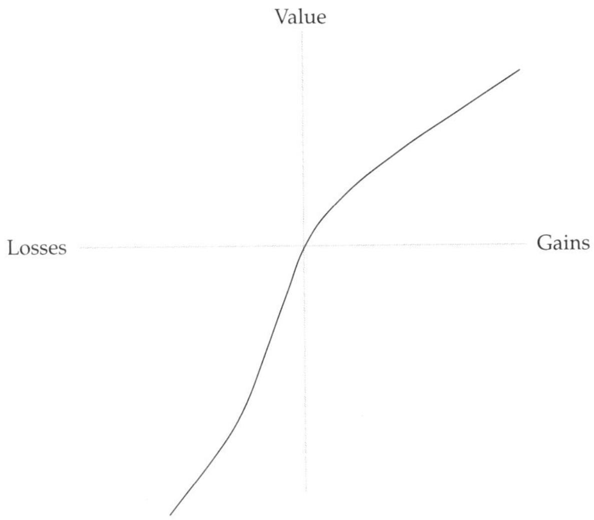


*Source*: Amos Tversky, based on data from Tversky and Kahneman (1986).

not have, classical economic theory does not address losses. The language of losses presupposes that people evaluate things relative to some reference point; so, the domain of this value function is gains and losses rather than wealth.

The second feature is that the value function is concave above the reference point and convex below it, which results in the characteristic S shape. This feature means that people are maximally sensitive to changes near the reference point: The first $1,000 gained is the most attractive, and the first $1,000 lost is the most unattractive. This observation is consistent with a great deal of research on perception and judgment. For example, the illumination inside a room at noon may be several orders of magnitude less than outside, yet the people in the room adjust to the inside level and see each other quite clearly. They are not aware that the room is dark in comparison with the street. However, they instantly notice even a small change in the brightness of the light in the room. The same is true for many dimensions of human experience, including monetary changes.

The third feature of the value function is that it is asymmetrical; the loss curve is much steeper than the gain curve. A loss appears larger to most people than a gain of equal size; a loss of, say, $5,000 is generally perceived to be much more aversive than a gain of $5,000 is attractive. This characteristic, called loss aversion, explains why most people are not willing to toss a fair coin to decide whether they will win or lose $100. Experiments show that faced with a 50/50 chance to win or lose, people require a potential gain of $200 to offset a potential loss of $100. In other words, a 50/50 chance to win $200 or lose $100 is barely acceptable to most people. Mark Twain put it best when he said, "Wives do not so much object to their husbands gambling. They object to their husbands losing." The losses, not the risk per se, are what drive people's preferences.

Loss aversion—the greater impact of the downside than the upside—is a fundamental characteristic of the human pleasure machine. Think of how well you feel today and use that as your reference point. You probably can think of days on which you were a little more energetic and felt a little better. Do you imagine things could be a great deal better or only slightly better? Now imagine how much worse they could be. You probably imagine things could be *slightly* better but *infinitely* worse. We have probably evolved to be very sensitive to losses and much less sensitive to gains.

People exhibit inconsistent attitudes toward risk. As noted earlier, most people are risk averse in gains and risk seeking in losses; they prefer a sure gain of $100 to a 50/50 chance to get $200 or nothing, and they prefer a 50/50 chance of losing $200 or nothing to a sure loss of $100. Now consider this experiment: People are given money before the game begins; they are to imagine themselves with $300 for the gain game and $500 for the loss game. In both cases, they have a choice between a sure $400 and a 50/50 chance to get either $300 or $500. Although the problems are now identical, people continue to exhibit risk-averse behavior in the gain problem and risk-seeking behavior in the loss problem. In short, people act differently depending on the "framing" of the problem; the perception of what is gained and what is lost can be manipulated by the way the outcomes are arranged.

The following example illustrates the kind of problems this tendency can produce in portfolio decisions. In a study, people had the following options:

*Decision I*

A. A sure gain of $240

B. A 25 percent chance to gain $1,000

*Decision II*

C. A sure loss of $750

D. A 75 percent chance to lose $1,000

Given the choice between A and B, 84 percent of the participants chose A; they preferred a sure gain of $240 to a 25 percent chance of winning $1,000. Given the choice between C and D, 87 percent chose D; they preferred a 75 percent chance of losing $1,000 to a sure loss of $750. Overall, 73 percent selected A and D and only 3 percent chose B and C. But consider the *aggregated* outcomes:

A&D = a 25 percent chance of gaining $240 and a 75 percent chance of losing $760

B&C = a 25 percent chance of gaining $250 and a 75 percent chance of losing $750.

Aggregating the decision outcomes makes evident that A&D is inferior to B&C, although the former was much more popular than the latter.

This example illustrates the consequences of the combination of risk aversion and risk seeking. People pay a premium to obtain a sure gain, and they pay a premium to avoid a sure loss. In combination, these actions lead to inferior choices. This example demonstrates that the tendency to make risk-averse choices in gains and to make risk-seeking choices in losses can cause people to choose suboptimal portfolios.

## Mental Accounting

People's preferences depend on their reference points, not on objective outcomes alone. Standard economic analysis assumes that people combine all relevant outcomes and make choices accordingly, but many behavioral phenomena are inconsistent with this assumption. Through a process of mental accounting, people construct systems of evaluation and combination of outcomes in their own minds that influence their choices.

In classical economic theory, money is fungible: A dollar is a dollar is a dollar. People, however, tend to organize their transactions in a way that makes money much less than wholly fungible. In many organizations, for example, various budget constraints make it possible to do one thing but not another, such as making photocopies but not long-distance phone calls. Similar constraints often operate within individuals, and these constraints are called mental accounting.

Mental accounting explains a lot of behavior. In the Decision I/Decision II problem, for example, most people evaluated the two problems as individual decisions rather than as a portfolio decision. The result was a suboptimal portfolio decision. For another example of mental accounting, suppose someone loses $100 in the morning and makes $100 in the afternoon. When evaluating the day, that person is likely to judge it a down day because the evaluation is likely to be made on a transaction-by-transaction basis and because the loss of $100 is more upsetting than the later gain of $100 is uplifting. If the person were to combine the transactions, he or she would realize it was not a bad day because money was neither lost nor made.

The following example is a variation of the problem. Imagine you have decided to see a play for which admission is $20 a ticket. When you arrive at the theater, you discover you have lost a $20 bill. Would you still pay $20 for the play? Most people say yes. Now imagine that you have purchased an admission ticket for $20 and, as you enter the theater, you discover that you have lost the ticket. Would you pay $20 for another ticket? Of course, the choice would depend on the real price and the person's level of income, but in tests, most people say no. Fewer than half are willing to pay $20 to buy another ticket.

Why are most people quite willing to pay $20 if they lose a $20 bill but not willing to pay another $20 if they lose the ticket? After all, there is no real difference between the two problems. So, why the different attitudes?

Evidently, people think of the problems differently. In the second case, the act of buying the ticket involves opening what might be called a "going-to-the-theater account." By the time the ticket is lost, this account is down $20, and buying a second ticket would mean a cost of $40. A person who considers the play probably worth $20 may not consider it worth $40, so that person does not buy the second ticket. In the case of the lost $20 bill, however, the money has not become part of the going-to-the-theater account. It is part of general accounting, so the lost $20 can be allocated to another account. The different internal accounting for the losses makes people behave differently.

This phenomenon is quite common. For example, many people save money for their children's college tuition, and many of these same families borrow money to buy a car at an interest rate that far exceeds the interest rate they receive on that college education account. Thus, unlike the classical economic conception that money is fungible and people move it from one place to another at will, behavioral finance recognizes that people have boundaries that control how transactions are organized and evaluated and what transactions are carried out.

## Overconfidence

Classical economic theory posits the notion of rational expectation: People are efficient information processors and act on that information. The classical theory does not assume that people know everything, but it does assume that they make good use of the information that is available to them and that their evaluation of the evidence is unbiased. Study after study indicates, however, that people's judgments are often erroneous—and in a very predictable way. People are generally overconfident. They acquire too much confidence from the information that is available to them, and they think they are right much more often than they actually are.

One of the earliest demonstrations of this phenomenon involved evaluations of the predictive power of interviews. Many people believe that they can make reasonable predictions about a person based on a brief interview, although much research indicates that this is not so. Nevertheless, superficial impressions often dominate people's behavior and are hard to shake.

Another example of overconfidence comes from the records of medical experts diagnosing medical conditions. A recent study of physicians showed that when they had 90 percent confidence in a diagnosis of pneumonia, they were right, on average, about 50 percent of the time.

Overconfidence seems to be built into humans, in the sense that the mind is probably designed to extract as much information as possible from what is available rather than to assess how little is known about a particular issue. Evaluation of stocks is no exception. In one recent study, security analysts were asked such questions as what is the probability that the price of a given stock will exceed $X by a given date. On average, analysts were 80 percent confident, but only 60 percent accurate, in their assessments.

In other studies, analysts were asked for their high and low estimates of the price of a given stock. The high estimate was to be a number they were 95 percent sure the actual value would fall below. The low estimate was to be a number they were 95 percent sure the actual would fall above. Thus, the high and low estimates should have bounded 90 percent of the cases, and if people were realistic or unbiased, the number of cases in which the actual price fell outside the range the experts gave—that is, either below the low estimate or above the high estimate—should have been 10 percent. In fact, the actual numbers fell outside the range about 35 percent of the time.

Rather than operating on rational expectations and unbiased estimates, people are commonly biased in several directions: They are optimistic; they overestimate the chances that they will succeed; and they overestimate their degree of knowledge, in the sense that their confidence far exceeds their hit rate.

Overconfidence has many implications. Perhaps the most obvious is that people should be careful in making predictions. Just because something seems correct does not mean it is correct. Overconfidence also may help explain excessive trading and a great deal of the volatility in the market. If each person has a limited amount of information and is confident that his or her predictions are right, the result is a great deal of trading, much more than would be expected under a rational model.

## Conclusion

The phenomena reviewed here involving risk attitudes, mental accounting, and overconfidence are based on psychological principles of judgment and choice that are clearly at variance with the general precepts of classical economic theory. These phenomena have three implications for behavioral finance. First, they indicate that the rational economic model that informs much of financial analysis is incomplete in some essential respects, and the departures are systematic rather than random. Second, they offer a way to explain many market anomalies and investor phenomena that are puzzling from a classical perspective. Third, an understanding of risk attitudes, mental accounting, and overconfidence may provide opportunities to exploit these biases in the market and improve investment strategies and performance.

# Question and Answer Session

Amos Tversky

**Question:** Given that analysts are not very good at estimating future earnings, should managers give up their earnings revision or earnings surprise models?

**Tversky:** This question relates to the predictability of the market, which is beyond the scope of this presentation. From the standpoint of the behavioral phenomena I discussed, analysts should be more skeptical of their ability to predict trends than they usually are. Time and time again, we learn that our confidence is misplaced, and our overconfidence leads to bad decisions, so recognizing our limited ability to predict the future is an important lesson to learn.

This conclusion is not limited to investment professionals. Lawyers, for example, tend to overestimate their probabilities of winning in court. If you ask both sides of a legal dispute who will win, each will say its chances of winning are greater than 50 percent. Perhaps a more realistic assessment of the situation would lead to better legal advice to clients and fewer court cases.

**Question:** Do men and women make different decisions when given the same set of facts?

**Tversky:** We have found little evidence of differences between men and women in decision making. Early research indicated that women are slightly less likely to take risks than men are, but later studies did not confirm that tendency. I don't know whether that difference in results was a function of changed methodology or a change in the culture between 1960 and 1990 (see also Harlow and Brown 1990).

**Question:** Do any of these cognitive biases change if people have a great deal of experience or if they have the opportunity to learn from experience—for example, from one game to the next in a study?

**Tversky:** Unfortunately, cognitive illusions are not easily unlearned. This is not to say that people do not learn from experience, but what is learned is often quite specific to a particular context and does not generalize to other contexts. The fact that in the real world people have not learned to eliminate framing, loss aversion, and overconfidence speaks for itself. Some hope exists for specific training, but we should not expect such training to be widely generalized.

**Question:** Does the inconsistent behavior that you describe occur in all cultures?

**Tversky:** Yes. There is evidence of these phenomena in several cultures, including Japan, China, and Europe. Some researchers have found similar phenomena even in animal behavior.

**Question:** Does time horizon affect people's thinking?

**Tversky:** Most of the problems I discussed here were not temporal, but the question is pertinent because myopia is common in human behavior. People tend to make decisions that appear right at a particular time or that represent their current view or their immediate conception; they have a tendency to avoid considering a long time horizon.

**Question:** Does any prevailing evolutionary theory explain why negative events—death, hunger—loom larger than positive events—live better, feel better, taste better?

**Tversky:** Evolutionary explanations are intriguing—and dangerous, because we can always make up a story that would explain why the data represent an optimal evolutionary path. I do believe, however, that the gain/loss asymmetry has an evolutionary basis, and it probably has to do with the fact that sensitivity to losses was probably more adaptive than the appreciation of gains. It would have been wonderful to be a species that was almost insensitive to pain and had an infinite capacity to appreciate pleasure. But you probably wouldn't have survived the evolutionary battle.

**Question:** What behavioral issues are currently being researched?

**Tversky:** Much current research is focusing on the psychology of judgment under uncertainty—understanding how people make judgments, how they assess uncertainty, and how they evaluate uncertain prospects. I am pleased to see that more and more psychological research is finding its way to the theory and practice of finance.

# Investor Psychology and the Dynamics of Security Prices

Werner F.M. De Bondt
*Frank Graner Professor of Investment Management*
*University of Wisconsin–Madison*

Economics is a science, but it is a social science; the human factor—particularly beliefs that shape how humans interpret and act on information—plays a substantial role in the behavior of financial markets. Four attributes of beliefs are important to keep in mind: (1) Most concepts and frameworks are shared. (2) Beliefs differ greatly in sophistication. (3) Beliefs are often false. (4) Beliefs do not change easily. From a practical point of view, by emphasizing the importance of individuals' decisions, the behavioral approach reaffirms that good business judgment is critical in money management.

Why should professional money managers, academicians, and other rational people spend their leisure time learning more about investor psychology? The answer is simple: Most of us would agree that the behavior of financial markets is often far from rational. Yet, despite extraordinary events here and overseas (e.g., the 1987 stock market crash), modern finance theory has almost completely ignored the complex motivational and cognitive factors that influence investor decision making. This presentation takes a different approach. First, I explain why psychology matters and why a behavioral approach is currently the most promising and exciting way to think about financial issues. Next, I briefly explore how the behavior of money managers, financial analysts, and individuals shapes the dynamics of stock prices—in particular, how investor sentiment sometimes causes price momentum and sometimes causes price reversals. The exploration requires a discussion of the links between stock price movements and economic fundamentals, trader perceptions of risk and return, and the "state of the market."

## The Practical Challenge

Investment managers care about the psychology of financial markets because they want to create wealth—for themselves and for their clients. To create wealth, they need to develop strategies that will be successful, and to develop strategies, they need to understand how markets operate. Logically, some positive theory of how the world works always comes prior to the development of normative principles. Thus, the place to start is with descriptions of what investors do, whether their actions seem sensible or not. From these descriptions derives a theory of market behavior.

What are the exact links between security prices and news—that is, value-relevant information? Over the decades, researchers have thought about this question in various ways. The basic issue is whether prices react properly to new information. In the past, three responses to this issue have emerged. The first defines the efficient markets hypothesis: "The price is right." That is, according to this centerpiece of modern finance theory, market prices adequately reflect all information at all times. The second response is that the relationship between prices and true intrinsic values does not exist; the market has a life of its own, and prices are driven by, in the words of John Maynard Keynes, "animal spirits." The third response, and the one that receives the most support from the empirical work in behavioral finance, resembles Isaac Newton's law of universal gravitation: What goes up must come down. Applied to the stock market, this law means that, over time, prices tend to revert to value. In the short term, however, big disparities may arise between the two.

These three perspectives on asset valuation have different implications for money management. The price-is-right answer suggests that "you can't beat the market" and that indexing is the way to go. The animal-spirits view is fascinated by the study of investor sentiment, initial public offering and growth stock fads, and technical analysis. Newton's law of gravity suggests pursuing fundamental analysis in the style of Benjamin Graham and David Dodd. Note that two of the three approaches recommend that investment professionals pay careful attention to human behavior.

## The Failures of Modern Finance

For 30 years, however, modern finance as taught in U.S. business schools has claimed the opposite—that human behavior is not important to the markets. Investors are invited to assume that markets and people are "perfect." The conduct of the representative agent (an ordinary Joe Sixpack), which is reflected in security prices, is described as the ideal type of *homo economicus*. The theory says, pure and simple, that people behave the way we would want them to behave. Because *homo economicus* is utterly and completely rational, all behavior is reduced to a mathematical optimization problem. Math is in; psych is out. Deduction is in; induction is out. Strictly analytical, quantitative methods—logically deduced from first principles—are the way to create value. Nuclear physicists and engineers know how to optimize; so, even without reading the social science literature, they must be great social scientists—and even better money managers.

Of course, no one can argue with the use of Reason, but any theory is only as good as its foundations: Garbage in, garbage out. So, from a practical point of view, how successful is modern finance? We can judge the theory by listing some of its main insights and testing how well they stand up to the data. Or we can judge the whole framework by what it leaves out and does not even attempt to explain (e.g., trading volume).

Following the first method, consider briefly three major ideas familiar to every student of modern finance: (1) The price of any asset equals the sum of the appropriately discounted expected cash flows; (2) risky assets sell at lower prices than risk-free assets (and risk is best measured by beta, or covariability); and (3) markets are efficient.

The fallacy of the discounted cash flow model as a descriptive theory of market prices was first exposed by Robert Shiller (1981a). Shiller compared actual stock prices with *ex post* rational prices—that is, prices calculated using the dividend discount model (DDM). After the fact, the DDM tells analysts what—with perfect foresight—a company should have been worth in, say, 1900. Shiller studied the S&P 500 Index between 1870 and 1979, and his findings are reproduced in **Figure 1**.

**Figure 1. Real S&P Composite Stock Price Index versus *Ex Post* Rational Price**

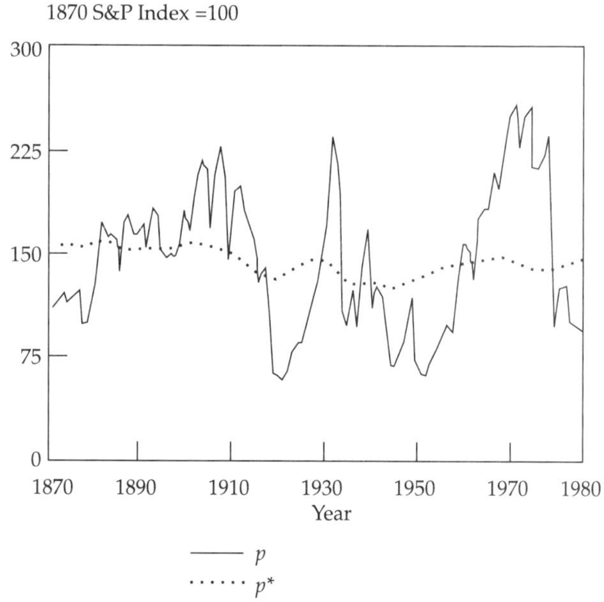


*Note*: Both lines have been detrended through dividing by a long-run exponential growth factor. The variable $p^*$ is the present value of actual subsequent real detrended dividends, subject to an assumption about the present value in 1979 of dividends thereafter.

*Source*: Shiller (1981a).

Figure 1 compares the *ex post* index with the actual index. The figure teaches three things. First, it shows that actual prices ($p$) are much more volatile than DDM-estimated prices ($p^*$). For example, in the Great Depression, markets crashed, but DDM-estimated prices for that period exhibit only a slight dip. Of course, market participants may have worried about scenarios of history much worse than what actually occurred, but the puzzle is why price volatility was for so long not validated by subsequent movements in dividends. As Shiller proved, the logic of DDM requires that the volatility in $p^*$ be larger than the volatility in $p$. The data, therefore, totally contradict the DDM theory.

The second implication of Figure 1 is that factors other than dividends (and the economic determinants of dividends) play a big role in price determination. This implication opens the door for investor psychology.

The third insight from Figure 1 (and perhaps the most troublesome for practitioners) is the implication it has for fundamental analysis. Even an analyst with perfect foresight, with a crystal ball, could deliver only DDM price estimates ($p^*$). But wealth is created by buying low and selling high. The conclusion must be that rational money managers cannot ignore market sentiment.

Recent research has further demonstrated the embarrassing weakness of our theories of the risk–return trade-off and efficient markets. For instance, the academic literature is replete with evidence of seasonality—short- and long-term predictability in returns. Even Eugene Fama has withdrawn his support for the celebrated Sharpe–Lintner–Black capital asset pricing model and its notion of beta risk. Today, our best pricing models say that, in the cross-section of stocks, the required return on equity moves with market capitalization and with the ratio of market value to book value, a number constructed by accountants. No one has any good story, however, to explain why it does. Thus, the sad but honest truth is that, despite its many insights, modern finance offers only a set of asset-pricing theories for which no empirical support exists and a set of empirical facts for which no theory exists.[1]

## The Theoretical Challenge

How should academicians react to this state of affairs? Familiar tunes often sung by theorists blame the data. "The data are noisy and cannot be trusted," theorists lament. "Measurement error, survivorship bias, selection bias," they sigh. If the data are numerous, "The data are mined." If the data are few, "The theory cannot be properly tested."

I do not like an approach that takes heart and derives its appeal from the fact that it cannot be falsified. Rather, I believe that the challenge is to develop new and better theories of asset pricing. Above all, the new theory should explain the joint puzzle of excess market volatility and excess trading. In my view, understanding of investor psychology is critical to this task.

Psychology influences prices so long as two conditions are fulfilled. Both are necessary. The first condition, that of "bounded rationality," is that people are human; Joe Sixpack is fallible. The second condition is that rational arbitrage is imperfect.

That people try their best but make mistakes, that people often repeat their mistakes, and that many people make the same mistakes—these everyday observations are beyond question. Because asset valuation is about the future, and because the future is unknown and in the distance, asset valuation is really about quality of judgment. In some fundamental way, finance is a branch of the psychology of judgment. Contrary to what some theorists may say, expectations are not always rational.

Why is arbitrage imperfect? One reason is that arbitrage is costly and there is no free lunch in information gathering. The usual arbitrage arguments also exclude true diversity of opinion. Consider, however: If an oil tanker in the Persian Gulf sinks, some traders will think that event is great news for Exxon Corporation while others will think it is terrible for Exxon. The price of Exxon will reflect how many dollars people are willing to put behind these two beliefs. Thus, false beliefs matter.

Another reason arbitrage is imperfect is that irrational traders create additional risk for themselves and everyone else. An analyst may find that some stock is undervalued and should be bought, but if other people do not come to the same belief within some reasonable period of time, arbitrage is not worthwhile and, in fact, the analyst may be hurt by unjustified price movements.

Finally, rational arbitrage may be destabilizing. If a rational person knew in advance that a television story rehashing old facts long known to sophisticated investors would be on the Thursday evening news and would cause the price of IBM to go up on Friday, what would that person do? Bet against the price rise because the news is old hat? Not at all. He or she would buy now, buy before the price increase. Thus, arbitrage can destabilize prices and make matters worse.

We have no choice but to take on the monumental job of modeling irrational "noise" traders. What people do affects prices and, therefore, affects everyone.

Clearly, this psychological approach is quite different from a perspective that emphasizes perfect markets and perfect people. It also contrasts with the neo-institutional paradigm. Modern institutionalists try to model market frictions, but they still regard the marginal trader to be fully rational. That is, to institutionalists, if information is asymmetrical—that is, if some people know more than others—the people who know less know that they know less and act in full recognition that they know less. The behaviorists, on the other hand, assume that the stupid (or less-informed people) are indeed stupid but do not know that they are stupid.

## Mental Frames

The effect of judgment on asset prices is a product of the beliefs (or mental frames) that traders, rightly or wrongly, share. The effect also depends on how traders incorporate new information into the frame. Because perceptions play such an important role, four attributes of beliefs are important to keep in mind.

First, people do not create many frames that are uniquely their own. Concepts and frameworks are shared. That is why we can speak over dinner about the war in Bosnia without ever having been there. Second, beliefs differ greatly in sophistication. If a

[1]Merton Miller seems to agree with this characterization. In a 1994 interview with *The Economist* (April 23), he said that "the blending of psychology and economics . . . is becoming popular simply because conventional economics has failed to explain how asset prices are set." The reasoning may be simple, but at least to me, it is convincing. Miller added, however, that he believes the new mix of psychology and finance "will lead nowhere."

passenger asks a taxi driver about the link between the budget deficit and interest rates, the likely response will be a confused look and a short, one-sentence answer. If the person were to ask a professional economist, her reply might take an hour—admittedly, perhaps with the same net effect as the taxi driver's answer. Third, beliefs are often false. Some years ago, I watched an afternoon television talk show about the savings and loan crisis. One of the people in the audience said, "The taxpayers shouldn't pay for this mess. The government should." Modern finance surely overestimates the sophistication of the public! In short, it is preposterous to assume, as rational expectations theorists do, that everyone has a superb understanding of how the macroeconomic and financial systems work. Finally, beliefs do not change easily. People have an enormous capacity to rationalize facts and fit them into a preexisting belief system. Inflationary expectations in the bond market demonstrate this point. One way to interpret the low returns on fixed-income instruments in the 1970s is that most investors never thought inflation would go up as much as it did. Similarly, the very high real returns experienced during the early 1980s may have resulted from the conviction that inflation was here to stay.

That shared beliefs affect market prices, often the wrong way, is evident from a careful study of business history. A good example is U.S. corporate restructuring. In retrospect, is it surprising that the merger and acquisition wave of the 1960s (when many firms diversified into new activities) was followed by the break-up wave of the 1980s and 1990s? A reasonable person might wonder if the initial M&A wave was largely in error. Profit data certainly suggest that it was. The management gurus of the 1960s loved diversification and saw it as a big plus for company value, whereas today, their buzzword is "focus." What is most striking, however, is that the stock market apparently took the gurus seriously, not once but twice: Event studies show that stock prices of bidder firms reacted favorably to acquisition news in the 1960s but unfavorably in the 1980s. It is rather perilous and bad practice to judge the value of a long-term investment decision by the whim of a short-term price reaction.

## Heuristics and the Dynamics of Security Prices

How do security prices respond to news? That depends in part on how investors' mental frames are influenced by new information. There are always two effects. The first has to do with the short-term impact of the surprising news in light of the information already impounded in prices. The second effect depends on how the news changes the frame itself. At times, seemingly minor pieces of news trigger a change in mental frame and lead to a big price reaction.

A major focus of my past research has been the quality of financial forecasts. How good are expert and amateur predictions of inflation, economic growth, company earnings, stock prices, etc.? In addition, how do people go about making these forecasts? A recurring theme is the tendency of most forecasters to extrapolate the immediate past. People seem to have a difficult time projecting anything greatly different from what is already happening. This tendency may be viewed as an "overreaction" to what is salient and obvious. Laboratory research indicates that non-Bayesian forecasting probably results from the use of mental heuristics, namely, representativeness, availability, and adjustment and anchoring (Tversky and Kahneman 1974).

Security analysts' earnings forecasts are a good example (De Bondt and Thaler 1990). The forecasts are persistently very wide of the mark. And notwithstanding their large errors, analysts keep offering extreme predictions. In addition, the data show optimism bias as well as serial correlation in forecast errors (Brown 1993). Somewhat similar phenomena are observed with stock price forecasts made by small individual investors. For several years, the American Association of Individual Investors has asked a random sample of its members for a stock market forecast every week. The data show that, just like subjects in controlled experiments, most individuals are optimistic in bull markets and pessimistic in bear markets. The forecasts, however, have little or no predictive power (De Bondt 1993).

A series of empirical tests supports the idea that overreaction bias affects stock prices (De Bondt and Thaler 1985). **Figure 2** summarizes the initial, and controversial, study of the winner/loser effect. Richard Thaler and I examined all companies listed on the NYSE since December 1925. As Figure 2 shows, the 50 NYSE stocks that did the worst during an initial

**Figure 2. The Returns to Buying Past Losers and Selling Past Winners Short**

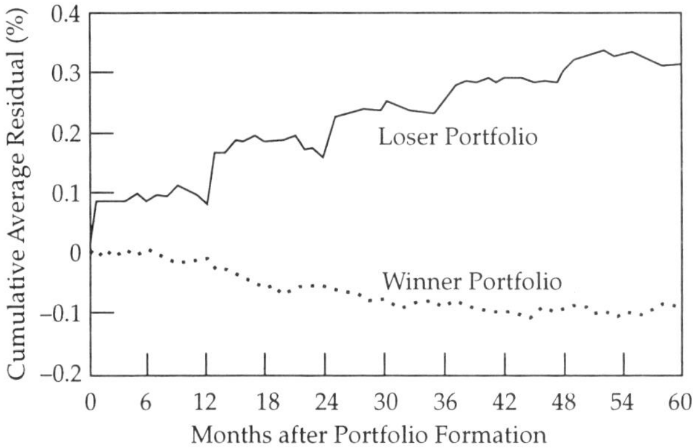


*Source*: Werner F.M. De Bondt, based on data from De Bondt and Thaler (1985).

50 NYSE stocks that did the worst during an initial five-year period subsequently outperformed the 50 NYSE stocks that did the best. Stock prices apparently "have a memory," because the difference in performance when one has controlled for time-varying risk and other factors is, on average, about 8 percent a year. Despite many attempts to refute these findings, they still stand. In fact, the seeming profitability of contrarian strategies of this type has been established for many different countries and time periods. The winner/loser effect was the first asset-pricing anomaly predicted and discovered by a behavioral theory.

What causes the winner/loser effect? My favorite behavioral explanation is that traders naively extrapolate past earnings trends. In a 1992 study, I tested this overreaction-to-earnings hypothesis. I wondered whether analysts' earnings forecasts could be used to earn abnormal profits. The period was 1976 through 1984, and I used more than 100,000 forecasts. Firms were ranked on the basis of analyst predicted earnings growth for one-, two-, and five-year horizons. Apparently, an arbitrage strategy that buys the 20 percent of companies for which analysts are most pessimistic and finances the purchases by selling short the 20 percent of companies for which analysts are most optimistic earns substantial profits. **Figure 3** shows the risk-adjusted excess returns for the 21 months following initiation of the strategy. Note that the longer the forecast period, the greater the excess returns. These findings—echoes of Newton's law of universal gravitation—strongly support the overreaction-to-earnings hypothesis and contrarian investment styles in general.

Plenty of mystery stories are left in the data. One puzzle is the empirical evidence documenting *underreaction*. **Figure 4** is taken from a survey on the topic by Victor Bernard (1993). If companies are ranked on the basis of standardized earnings surprises (surrounding the day of their earnings announcements), companies with positive earnings news are much better subsequent investments than are companies that report bad news. The effect lasts for many months and, surprisingly, the strategy has consistently paid off for more than a quarter of a century.

How do we square the overreaction results with the underreaction results? How do we square price momentum with price reversals? Logically, can both be true? The answer is a definite yes. Large disparities between price and value can result from the wrong mental frame. For example, we freely talk about "growth firms" and "declining industries" even though annual earnings changes provide little evidence of any reliable time-series patterns (except in the tails of the distribution). All too often, the life-cycle metaphor proves persuasive. No wonder, then, that when an earnings surprise hits, many investors refuse to believe it. Mental frames and prices take time to adjust, and this slow adjustment may be responsible for the underreaction evidence. Another finding consistent with this overall interpretation of the data is that past stock market losers are more likely than not to experience positive earnings surprises and past market winners to report negative

**Figure 3. The Returns to Buying Companies with Poor Earnings Prospects and Selling Companies with Good Earnings Prospects**

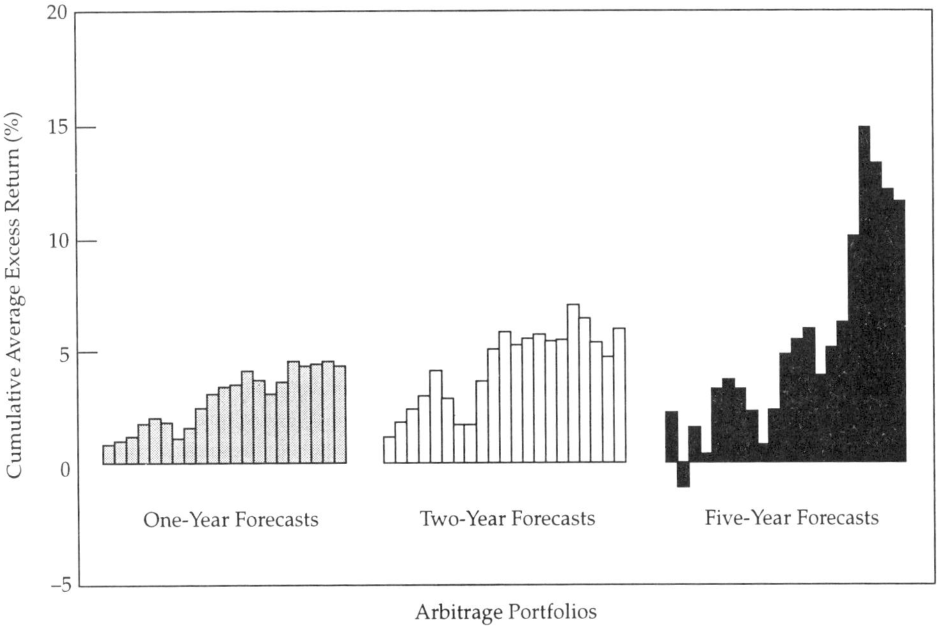


*Source*: De Bondt (1992).

**Figure 4. Returns to a Strategy Based on Standardized Unexpected Earnings: Results Reported in Three Studies**

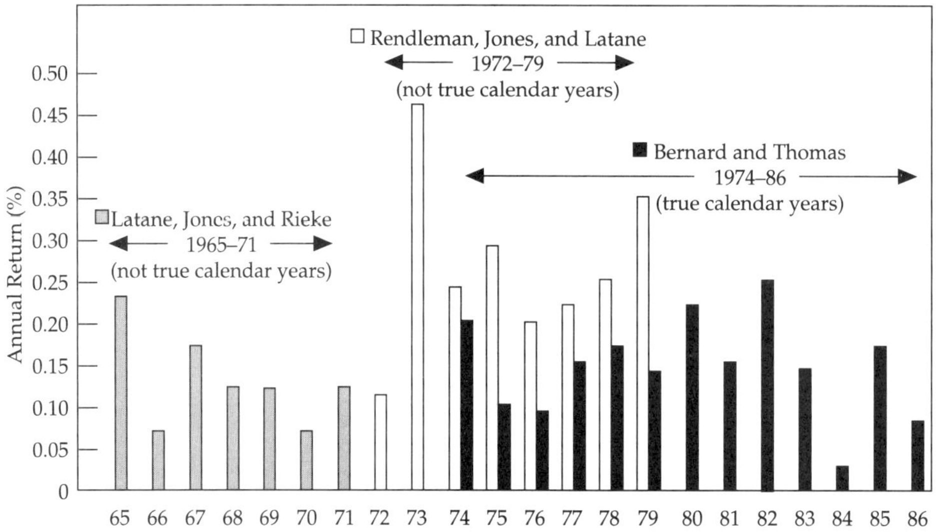


*Note*: For specific study descriptions and test assumptions, see Latane, Jones, and Rieke (1974), Rendleman, Jones, and Latane (1982), and Bernard and Thomas (1989).

*Source*: Bernard (1993).

surprises.

## Conclusion

In many ways, modern neoclassical finance has been notably successful in the past 30 years. Consider, for instance, the impact of the Black–Scholes option-pricing formula. Yet, while we take pride in financial economics as a science, we should never forget that it is a social science. The human factor plays a substantial role in the behavior of financial markets.

U.S. economist John Maurice Clark understood this connection well. He stated in 1918 that

> . . . the economist may attempt to ignore psychology, but it is sheer impossibility for him to ignore human nature. . . . If the economist borrows his conception of man from the psychologist, his constructive work may have some chance of remaining purely economic in character. But, if he does not, he will not thereby avoid psychology. Rather, he will force himself to make his own, and it will be bad psychology.

Unfortunately, modern finance involves a lot of bad psychology.

Fortunately, behavioral finance is a call for more discipline in financial modeling. Before we make further arbitrary, *ad hoc* assumptions (such as rational expectations or Bayesian updating), perhaps we should check with our colleagues in the arts and sciences as to whether any evidence exists that people behave according to the assumptions.

From a practical point of view, the behavioral approach reaffirms that good business judgment is critical—in money management as in everything else. Something useful derives from the study of heuristics and biases and from understanding how people process data and solve problems. The financial arena contains no shortcuts, however, no simple ways to get rich quick (except, perhaps, with privileged inside information). Whether long-term fundamental analysis pays off is still somewhat unclear. In all likelihood, the best approach is to live by Newton's law. All the evidence that I know warns against buying glamour, against buying companies with astronomical P/Es or highfliers in the stock market. Similarly, all the evidence I know finds wealth (if not virtue) in contrarian investing, in going against the crowd.

# Question and Answer Session

Werner F.M. De Bondt

**Question:** If a good strategy is simply to buy the 20 stocks with the most pessimistic earnings forecasts and sell the 20 with the most optimistic forecasts, what of the role of financial analysts?

**De Bondt:** Analysts have a useful role, but their position is certainly paradoxical. On the one hand, believers in efficient markets must explain what tens of thousands of analysts around the world do that is worth that much money. Why do analysts get paid if their insights are worthless? So, the survival of analysts is a puzzle within the rational paradigm.

On the other hand, believers in the competing view that market prices are often irrational are also in an uncomfortable position. If prices are irrational, why don't more professional investors outperform the indexes?

In the end, the success of the security analysis industry may reflect more what people *think* analysts are worth than what value analysts can really add. We all know that investors chase the celebrities who appear on the covers of *Business Week*, *Money* magazine, and so on. Of the many reasons for this investor behavior, the main one is the difficulty in distinguishing luck from skill. Extrapolation bias and overconfidence also play a role, however. Overconfident investors firmly believe that they themselves can outperform the market, even if others can't, or that they can pick somebody who will beat the averages for them.

**Question:** In your 1992 analyst forecast study, where was the money made—on the short side or the long side?

**De Bondt:** One aspect of the return data that we have not quite explained is that, in many overreaction studies, more of the profits seem to come from buying losers than from selling winners short. The ratio is about two to one. I am as much surprised at that finding today as I was ten years ago. When Thaler and I started this research, I thought picking a stock that is overpriced would be a lot easier than picking one that is underpriced. Much of the profit of contrarian strategies, however, comes from the loser side.

**Question:** Do noise traders become smarter over time? What can we do to improve our own judgment?

**De Bondt:** The efficient markets hypothesis implies not only that the smart cannot outperform the averages but that, as long as they are diversified, the stupid cannot underperform. Picking a portfolio that does worse than the S&P 500 is just as onerous as picking one that does better. So, uninformed investors can ride free on efficient market prices and be protected.

The evidence I have presented suggests a different model of financial markets, one in which wealth flows from the poorly informed to the well informed. Can this process last? I don't see why not. Foolishness characterizes all times and all places. Centuries ago, Erasmus of Rotterdam wrote a book called *In Praise of Folly*, and history shows that irrationality, prejudice, and superstition are pervasive. I have deep doubts about the rationalist philosophy of the Enlightenment that lurks behind neoclassical economics.

**Question:** What can we do to improve our own judgment?

**De Bondt:** Overcoming our natural biases is not easy, but a better awareness of the intuitive ways in which people look at problems can help. People should learn as much as they can about decision making—by, for instance, making themselves familiar with the laboratory research of psychology professors Amos Tversky and Daniel Kahneman or by reading the memoirs of important political and business leaders.

**Question:** Technical analysis seems to take behavioral biases into account. Why don't more people use technical analysis?

**De Bondt:** Behavioral finance and technical analysis agree on the relevance of investor psychology for asset pricing. The two approaches differ, however, in that technical analysis is the arena of practitioners and has not really gone through the rigors of scientific testing. Behavioral finance is part of science. Its adherents start from fundamental behavioral axioms (such as loss aversion or overreaction to salient news) and ask whether the theory built on the axioms can explain the stylized facts around us. Finally, they perform empirical tests to check the theory's predictive power out of sample. Thus, behavioral finance is much more rigorous than technical analysis.

# Behavioral Finance versus Standard Finance

Meir Statman
*Professor, Department of Finance*
*Leavey School of Business*
*Santa Clara University*

Behavioral finance is built on the framework of standard finance but supplies a replacement for standard finance as a descriptive theory. Behavioral finance reflects a different model of human behavior and is constructed of different components—prospect theory, cognitive errors, problems of self-control, and the pain of regret. These components help make sense of the world of finance—including investor preferences, the design of modern financial products, and financial regulations—by making sense of normal investor behavior.

Finance practitioners and academics are, or should be, interested in the following questions:

- Why do investors like dividends?
- Why do investors hate to realize losses?
- Why do investors prefer stocks of "good" companies?
- How are expected returns determined?
- What kinds of securities do investors like?
- What are the forces that shape financial regulations?

The range of questions is wide. It includes investor behavior; the interaction of investors in markets, which determines security prices; and the interaction of citizens in public policy arenas, which determines financial regulations.

Standard finance—the body of knowledge that is built on such pillars as the arbitrage principles of Merton Miller and Franco Modigliani, the portfolio construction principles of Harry Markowitz, the capital asset pricing theory of John Lintner and William Sharpe, and the option-pricing theory of Fischer Black, Myron Scholes, and Robert Merton—is so compelling because it uses only a few basic components to build a unified theory, a theory that should provide answers to all the questions of finance.

Few theories, however, are fully consistent with all the available empirical evidence, and standard finance is no exception. For example, Miller (1986) readily acknowledges that the observed preference for cash dividends is one of the "soft spots in the current body of theory" (p. S451). Miller goes on to argue, however:

> that the rationality-based market equilibrium models in finance in general and of dividends in particular are alive and well—or at least in no worse shape than other comparable models in economics at their level of aggregation. The framework is not so weighed down with anomalies that a complete reconstruction (on behavioral/cognitive or other lines) is either needed or likely to occur in the near future. (p. S466)

I argue that, today, ten years after Miller spoke, standard finance is indeed so weighted down with anomalies that it makes much sense to continue the reconstruction of financial theory on behavioral lines.

Standard finance is constructed with a few common components that have many uses. So is behavioral finance. But the components of standard finance and behavioral finance, reflecting different models of human behavior, are different. This presentation provides examples of the construction of behavioral finance as a framework that builds on standard finance and replaces it.

Proponents of standard finance often concede that their financial theory does poorly as a descriptive, or positive, theory of the behavior of individuals. They retreat to a second line of defense: that standard finance does well as a descriptive theory of the equilibrium that results from the interaction of individuals in markets. For example, Miller (1986) wrote that, for individual investors,

> stocks are usually more than just the abstract "bundles of returns" of our economic models. Behind each holding may be a story of family business, family quarrels, legacies received, divorce settlements, and a host of other considerations almost totally irrele-

vant to our theories of portfolio selection. That we abstract from all these stories in building our models is not because the stories are uninteresting but because they may be too interesting and thereby distract us from the pervasive market forces that should be our principal concern. (p. S467)

Even the second line of defense, however, does not hold. Evidence is mounting that the capital asset pricing model (CAPM), the market equilibrium theory by which risk and expected returns are determined in standard finance, is not a good description of reality. Moreover, contrary to Miller's view, I think that financial decisions by individuals and institutions are the proper domain of finance, not merely stories that "distract us from the pervasive market forces that should be our principal concern." Indeed, a good theory of the financial behavior of individuals is crucial for a good theory of the equilibrium that results from the interactions of individuals in the marketplace. To understand the differences between the components from which standard finance and behavioral finance are constructed, consider the arbitrage principle.

People in standard finance are not confused by frames. The pricing of a call option in the Black–Scholes model is a good example. The price of a call option is determined by substance: the knowledge that the cash flows of an option can be replicated by a particular dynamic combination of a bond and the underlying stock. The fact that in one case the cash flows are framed in terms of options and in the second case flows are framed in terms of bonds and stocks does not matter to standard finance investors. If the option cash flows exceed the cash flows of the stocks and bonds, "standard investors" engage in arbitrage, make arbitrage profits, and move prices to equilibrium levels where arbitrage is no longer profitable.

Whereas standard investors are never affected by frames, "behavioral investors" are often affected by frames. Moreover, behavioral investors are affected by frames in a normal, predictable way. Consider the following question: Which investment position is more risky?

1. a $1,000 long position in U.S. T-bills or
2. a $1,000 short position in naked call options on the S&P 500 Index.

Most people choose the options position as the more risky one. Someone whose overall portfolio is positively correlated with the S&P 500 and who has chosen the options position as the more risky position is probably a behavioral investor—one who has been fooled by the frame. The options position is negatively correlated with this investor's portfolio; thus, it provides a hedge and lowers overall portfolio risk. In contrast, the T-bill position has only a zero correlation with the portfolio and reduces its risk by less than the options position. Normal behavior is to ignore covariances and assess the risk of an asset in isolation from the overall portfolio. By that rule, the options position *is* more risky, but by the rules of Markowitz, the cash position is the more risky one.

People in standard finance are rational. People in behavioral finance are normal. When offered a choice between a $10 bill and a $20 bill, both rational and normal people choose the $20 bill. Rational people, however, are never confused by frames that make that $10 bill look like a $100 bill, whereas as Amos Tversky shows, normal people are often confused by frames.[1]

The effect of frames on choice is one part of Kahneman and Tversky's (1979) prospect theory, and prospect theory is one of the components of behavioral finance. Susceptibility to cognitive errors is a second component of behavioral finance (see Kahneman, Slovic, and Tversky 1982). For example, standard investors are never fooled by the "law of small numbers." They know that five years of return data on a mutual fund provide little information about the investment skills of the fund's manager. Standard investors also know that, as they assess the ability of the manager of a particular fund—say, the Magellan Fund—they should take into consideration the evidence on the ability of the average fund manager to beat the market. Behavioral investors tend to conclude that a five-year record of a fund is plenty of evidence about the skills of its manager and that the performance of the average fund manager is irrelevant in the assessment of the skill of a particular fund manager.

Standard-finance people are immune to problems of self-control. They stick to their diet plans and find it easy to turn down tempting desserts. They also stick to their savings plans and never engage in impulse buying. Behavioral investors are subject to temptation and, as Thaler and Shefrin (1981) noted, they look for ways to improve their self-control.

Standard-finance investors are also immune to the pain of regret (see Kahneman and Tversky 1982). Standard-finance people feel no greater disappointment when they miss their plane by a minute as when they miss it by an hour. Behavioral investors know the joy of pride and the pain of regret as they kick themselves harder when they miss the plane by only a minute.

The following sections describe how the components of prospect theory, cognitive errors, self-control, and regret can help make sense of the world of finance and answer the questions posed at the beginning of this presentation. I begin with dividends, the issue discussed by Miller (1986).

[1]See Professor Tversky's presentation, pp. 2–5.

## Investor Preferences for Cash Dividends

During the energy crisis of the early 1970s, Con Edison, the power company in New York City, decided to eliminate its dividend. At Con Edison's 1974 annual meeting, shareholders revolted; some cried, some had to be restrained from doing physical harm to the company's chairman. Here is a typical shareholder reaction, quoted from the transcript of the 1974 meeting:

> A lady came over to me a minute ago, and she said to me, "Please say a word for the senior citizens." And she had tears in her eyes. And I really know what she means by that. She simply means that now she will get only one check a month, and that will be her Social Security, and she's not going to make it because you have denied her that dividend.

Standard-finance shareholders of Con Edison would have been upset by the energy crisis and its impact on the value of Con Edison's stock, but they would not have been angry about the decision to eliminate the dividend. The Con Edison shareholders must have been behavioral investors.

Standard investors follow the arbitrage principle of Miller and Modigliani and know that in a world without taxes and transaction costs, they should be indifferent between a dollar in dividends and a dollar in capital. Standard investors are indifferent between dividends and capital because they do not rely on company decisions to create dividends. They can create "homemade dividends" by selling shares. Moreover, in a world where dividends are taxed more heavily than capital gains, investors are actually better off when companies refrain from paying dividends. So, why do investors like dividends? This is the puzzle to standard finance about which Black (1976) wrote. Hersh Shefrin and I have used the components of behavioral finance to explain why investors like dividends (Shefrin and Statman 1984).

A central element of prospect theory is that people segment their money into mental accounts. A dividend dollar is identical to a capital dividend in standard finance, but a dollar dividend is different from a capital dollar in prospect theory because the two dollars belong to separate mental accounts and mental accounting is done account by account. The decline in the price per share of Con Edison is a loss in the capital mental account, and the elimination of the dividend is a loss in the dividend mental account. Paying the dividend would have provided a "silver lining" lessening the pain even if the dividend payment had resulted in a further decline in the price of the stock.

Segregating monies into mental accounts is especially beneficial for people who have difficulty with self-control. As noted earlier, standard finance investors have no self-control difficulties in either diets or savings, but behavioral investors have to combat the desire for dessert even when they know that vegetables are better for their long-term welfare. Rules are a good tool for self-control. "No dessert before vegetables" is one such rule. "Consume from dividends but don't dip into capital" is another. Recall that the person who spoke for the woman at the Con Edison meeting did not even consider the possibility of dipping into capital to create homemade dividends.

Indeed, following standard finance theory can get people into deep trouble. One person in the audience at the Con Edison meeting asked why stock dividends were not paid in place of cash dividends "so at least the blow to stockholders by the omission of dividends would have been much less." The chairman, in an explanation that would have made Miller and Modigliani proud, explained that stock dividends are no more than pieces of paper and that shareholders can create homemade dividends by selling a few shares. The chairman missed the point entirely. Naming the pieces of paper "dividends" moves them from the capital mental account to a dividend mental account and allows consumption without violating the rule of "don't dip into capital."

In short, contrary to the precepts of standard finance, investors make important distinctions between dividends and capital. The distinctions are rooted in the way they frame money in mental accounts and the rules by which they use these frames to control savings and consumption. One cannot solve the dividend puzzle while ignoring the patterns of normal investor behavior.

## Selling Winners Too Early, Riding Losers Too Long

Underlying the arbitrage principle of Miller and Modigliani is the mechanism of arbitrage. An investor who sells a share at $100 in one market and simultaneously buys a share of the same company in another market for $95 engages in arbitrage, with a risk-free gain of $5. Of course, standard-finance investors never leave arbitrage opportunities unexploited.

The tax law, especially as it stood before the 1986 changes, provided investors with the "timing" arbitrage opportunity described by Constantinides (1983, 1984). The opportunity arises from differences in the tax rates on long-term and short-term gains and losses. Here is how it works: Imagine that you have $10,000 and you have decided to invest it in a no-load mutual fund, Fund A. You also identify Mutual Fund B, whose returns are perfectly correlated with the returns on Fund A. Imagine also that the "short term" is classified by the Internal Revenue Service as one year, so gain and loss realizations after one year are classified by the IRS as "long term."

You hold Fund A for a month, and as it happens, the stock market declines and your shares are now worth $9,000, a paper loss of $1,000. Now the arbitrage game at the expense of the IRS begins. You realize the $1,000 paper loss by selling your shares in Fund A and using the $9,000 in proceeds to buy shares of Fund B. The $1,000 loss, as a short-term loss, can be offset against your regular income taxed at, say, 30 percent. Your "rebate" from the IRS is 30 percent of $1,000, or $300. Now, imagine that you hold the $9,000 in Fund B for a year and a day, and the value of the shares appreciates from $9,000 to $10,000. You realize your $1,000 paper gain as a long-term gain. You pay, say, 20 percent, or $200, as a long-term tax to the IRS and buy $10,000 in shares of Fund A.

Compare your situation to the situation of an investor who held Fund A for the entire period. That investor begins with $10,000 and ends with $10,000—no gains, no losses. You, however, have $10,100 because your initial $300 tax rebate is $100 higher than the later $200 tax payment. This kind of arbitrage is easy. It involves only the exploitation of a quirk in the tax law. And, of course, standard-finance investors have no difficulty recognizing or exploiting arbitrage opportunities.

Behavioral investors have a problem with the arbitrage prescription; it requires the realization of a $1,000 "paper loss" as they sell Fund A and buy Fund B. Behavioral investors hate to realize losses. Behavioral investors think of money within mental accounts and distinguish paper losses from "realized losses." A stock with a paper loss might rise in price, so the chance exists that the mental account containing the stock will break even, but a realized loss means kissing the hope of breaking even goodbye. Behavioral investors are reluctant to realize losses, despite the tax advantages of doing so, because of the pain of regret that comes with kissing hope goodbye.

Gross (1982) described the reluctance of investors to realize losses this way:

> Many clients, however, will not sell anything at a loss. They do not want to give up the hope of making money on a particular investment, or perhaps they want to get even before they get out. The "getevenitis" disease has probably wrought more destruction on investment portfolios than anything else. (p. 150)

Shefrin and I have analyzed transactions in mutual funds and stocks and found evidence against the standard finance hypothesis that people engage in the tax arbitrage that Constantinides described (Shefrin and Statman 1985). Ignoring arbitrage opportunities and leaving $100 (or much more) in the pocket of the IRS may not be rational, but it is hard for behavioral investors to bring themselves to realize losses.

## Why Investors Prefer Stocks of Good Companies

Everyone has heard that beta is dead. Some say it is coming back; others say it is dead for good. The life or death of beta is so important because beta is the center of the CAPM and the CAPM is the standard-finance way of understanding risk, expected returns, and the relationship between the two.

The current state of the CAPM illustrates the danger in the tendency of standard finance to downplay an understanding of human behavior and concentrate instead on the resulting equilibrium in financial markets. The assumptions about human behavior that underlie the CAPM are not simplified versions of observed behavior. Rather, they contradict observed behavior. For example, investors in the world of the CAPM are assumed to agree on the expected returns of all assets. Of course, nobody believes that this assumption comes even close to a description of human behavior.

Assumptions about individual behavior might not matter when a theory works, but the CAPM does not work. Now that Fama and French (1992) have brought the sorry state of the CAPM to the headlines, standard finance offers no fallback theory for expected returns and risk. Instead, the result is data mining in the form of size and book-to-market effects.

Shefrin and I have also observed the choices of investors, rather than stock prices, and offered insights into the process by which investors form expectations about stock returns (Shefrin and Statman 1995b). An analysis of investor expectations might well be the best route to understanding the equilibrium levels of expected returns because, as everyone agrees, realized-return data, upon which virtually all current analyses are based, are very noisy. In comparison, the noise level in expectational data is low.

For example, *Fortune* magazine collects data on expectations through surveys it conducts of a group of respondents who are commonly regarded as sophisticated investors—executives, members of boards of directors, and financial analysts. Thousands of respondents are asked each year to rank companies on eight attributes, including quality of management, quality of products and services, and value as a long-term investment. The top three companies, as judged by the average quality score in the survey published in the February 1993 issue of *Fortune*, are Merck & Company, Rubbermaid, and Wal-Mart. The bottom three companies are Wang Laboratories, Continental Airlines, and Glenfed.

Consider the relationship between the rating of a given company on quality of management and on value as a long-term investment. Quality of management is an attribute of the *company*. In contrast, value as a long-term investment is an attribute of the *stock* of the company. If respondents to the *Fortune* survey believe in market efficiency, they will conclude that the price of a stock fully reflects the quality of the company. In efficient markets, the wonderful growth opportunities of good companies are fully reflected in the prices of their stocks, and therefore, the stocks offer no special value as a long-term investment. Similarly, the lousy growth opportunities of bad companies are fully reflected in the prices of their stocks. Neither stocks of good companies nor stocks of bad companies are bargains in an efficient market. If so, we should find a zero correlation between the *Fortune* ratings on quality of management and the *Fortune* ratings on value as a long-term investment.

Now consider, in contrast, what might be expected if the Fortune respondents are standard-finance investors who properly incorporate the knowledge reflected in findings on size and ratio of book value to market value (BV/MV) by Fama and French (1992) and others. Shefrin and I have found that, in general, companies that Fortune respondents rate highly by quality of management have high market values of equity (large size) and low BV/MVs. These characteristics, of course, apply to companies whose stocks provide low returns, according to Fama and French. If respondents to the Fortune survey are aware of the Fama and French results, explicitly or implicitly, they should produce a negative correlation between the rating of a company on quality of management and the rating of the stock of the company on value as a long-term investment. In fact, Shefrin and I found neither the zero correlation between quality of management and value as a long-term investment, which would be expected if the *Fortune* respondents believe stock prices are efficient, nor the negative correlation expected if the *Fortune* respondents follow Fama and French. Instead, we found a strong positive correlation. A regression of value as a long-term investment on quality of management produces not only a positive coefficient with a rare significant $t$-statistic, 43.95, but also an adjusted $R^2$ of 0.86. In other words, people as sophisticated as the *Fortune* respondents think that good stocks are the stocks of good companies although the evidence indicates that the opposite is true.

Why do people think that stocks of companies such as Merck, Rubbermaid, and Wal-Mart offer higher values as long-term investments than stocks of companies such as Wang, Continental Airlines, and Glenfed? Michael Solt and I have argued that investors tend to believe that good stocks are stocks of good companies because they fall prey to the *representativeness* heuristic (Solt and Statman 1989).

A person who follows the representativeness heuristic evaluates the probability of an uncertain event by the degree to which it (1) is similar in essential properties to its parent population and (2) reflects the salient features by which it is generated. In other words, an event A is judged more probable than an event B when A appears more representative than B. Kahneman and Tversky (1972) have supported the hypothesis that subjects judge the probability of an event by its representativeness with a series of experiments.

Consider this experiment (Kahneman and Tversky 1982). Subjects were presented with a brief personality sketch of Linda: Linda is 31 years old, single, outspoken, and very bright. She majored in philosophy. As a student, she was deeply concerned with issues of discrimination and social justice and also participated in antinuclear demonstrations.

Subjects were then asked which event is more probable:

- Linda is a bank teller (T).
- Linda is a bank teller and is active in the feminist movement (T & F).

The description of Linda was constructed to be similar to or representative of the profile of an active feminist and unrepresentative of that of a bank teller. Now, the rules of probability state that the compound event T & F cannot be more probable than the simple event T. Yet, 87 percent of all subjects judged the probability of the compound event that Linda is a bank teller *and* is active in the feminist movement as higher than the probability of the simple event that Linda is a bank teller.

The outcome of this experiment is consistent with the hypothesis that subjects judge the probability of an event by its similarity or representativeness. Specifically, because a feminist attitude seems more representative of Linda than the bank teller occupation, subjects concluded that Linda is more probably a bank teller and feminist than a bank teller.

In interviews following the experiment, Kahneman and Tversky asked 36 subjects to explain their choices. More than two-thirds of subjects who selected the compound event gave some version of a similarity or typicality argument as their reason but agreed, after some reflection, that the response was wrong because everyone who is both a bank teller and a feminist must also be a bank teller. Only two of the subjects maintained that the probability order need not agree with class inclusion, and only one claimed that he had misinterpreted the question.

In relation to good companies and good stocks, Solt and I argue that investors overestimate the probability that the stock of a good company is a good stock because they rely on the representativeness heuristic. They overestimate the probability that a good stock is stock of a good company because a good stock is similar to a good company.

The *Fortune* respondents rate stocks as if they like stocks of companies with high-quality management, with high market values of equity, and with low BV/MVs. Do they care about beta? No. Regression results show that there is no statistically significant relationship between value as a long-term investment and beta.

Typical *Fortune* respondents are behavioral investors, investors who believe that good stocks are stocks of good companies. Standard investors know what Fama and French know, that good stocks are stocks of bad companies. Behavioral investors load up on stocks of good companies. Standard investors tilt their portfolios toward stocks of bad companies, but being fully rational, they are mindful of the negative effect that concentration has on portfolio diversification. Thus, standard investors moderate the tilt toward stocks of bad companies, and the force that they exert on stock prices may not, therefore, be sufficient to counter fully the effect of behavioral investors. In short, the picture of equilibrium that Shefrin and I see consists of many behavioral investors who hold portfolios tilted toward the stocks of good companies, a few standard investors who hold portfolios tilted toward stocks of bad companies, and an expected-returns equilibrium where stocks of bad companies—low market values of equity and high BV/MVs—have high returns.

## The Design and Marketing of Financial Products

In teaching students the basics of options, I draw profit diagrams, as shown in **Figure 1**, of the four basic positions: buying a call, selling a call, buying a put, and selling a put. I ask the students, "Which positions do you like?" They like the idea of buying calls and puts, but they hate the idea of selling (naked) calls and puts. They explain that buying a call is attractive because the position has a floor on losses but unlimited potential for gains. "The maximum that I can lose is the premium," they say. Selling a (naked) call involves a ceiling on gains but unlimited potential for losses.

Next, I show them a profit diagram of a covered-call option (shown in **Figure 2**), a position that combines buying a share of stock for, say, \$21 and selling a call option on the stock with an exercise price of \$25 for \$1. My students like the idea of covered calls, but they are surprised to realize that the shape of the profit diagram of the covered-call position that they like is identical to the shape of the selling a (naked) put position that they hate. My students are hardly unique; the attraction of covered calls has been a puzzle to standard finance for years. But Shefrin and I have attempted to explain that attraction (Shefrin and Statman 1993a).

Covered calls are promoted by investment advisors as positions that contain free lunches. Here is an example from the Research Institute of America's

**Figure 1. Profit Diagram for Call and Put Options**

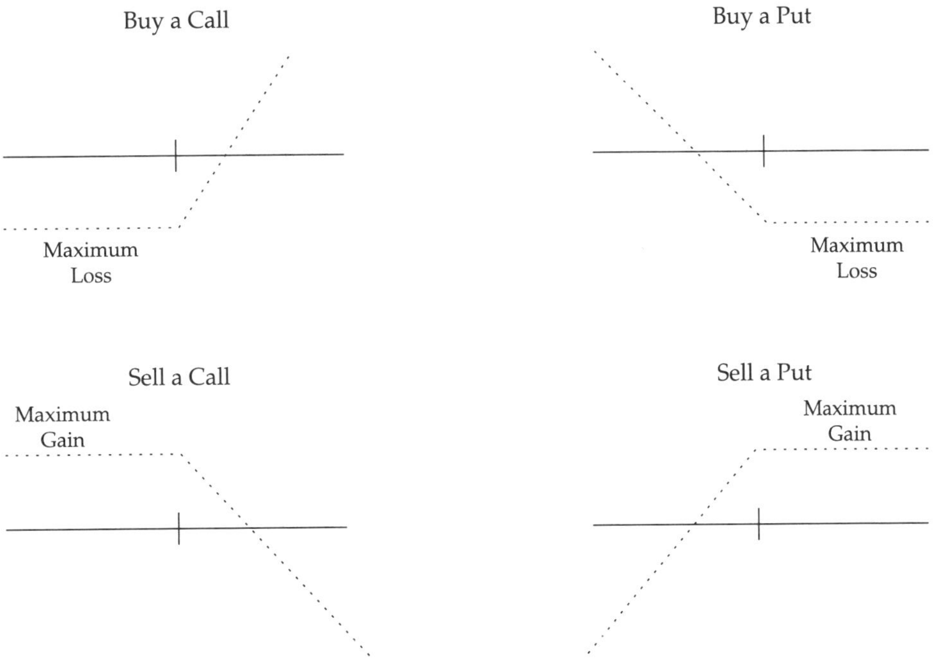


*Note*: The solid horizontal line in each diagram is the stock price at option expiration date. The tick marks on this line indicate the point at which the strike price equals the stock price at expiration.

*Source*: Meir Statman.

**Figure 2. Profit Diagram for a Covered-Call**

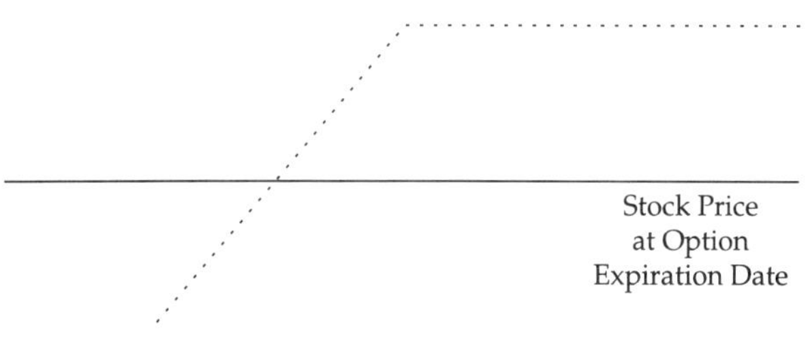


*Source*: Meir Statman.

*Personal Money Guide*:

> An investment strategy that can make you extra money is writing calls on securities you already own. . . . When you sell a call on a stock you own, you receive a premium. Think of these premiums as extra dividends. By careful selection of stocks and timing of writing calls, you have the opportunity to earn annual rates of returns of 11 percent to 19 percent: regular dividends of 4 percent to 9 percent and premium "dividends" of 7 percent to 10 percent.

And here is an example of the exasperated response of standard finance:

> Even for long-term investors who plan "never" to sell their stocks, the premiums received from writing options against these stocks cannot be treated as simply extra income to be added to the normal return of the stocks, as some advertising in the options industry seems to suggest. (Merton, Scholes, and Gladstein 1978)

Why do investors continue to ignore the good advice of standard finance? One part of the answer is that behavioral investors frame the cash flows of covered calls into separate mental accounts rather than integrate them as standard finance suggests. Consider the way Gross (1982) frames covered calls in his manual for brokers:

> Joe Salesman: You have told me that you have not been too pleased with the results of your stock market investments.
>
> John Prospect: That's right. I am dissatisfied with the return, or lack of it, on my stock portfolio.
>
> Joe Salesman: Starting tomorrow, how would you like to have three sources of profit every time you buy a common stock?
>
> John Prospect: Three profit sources? What are they?
>
> Joe Salesman: First, you could collect a lot of dollars—maybe hundreds, sometimes thousands—for simply agreeing to sell your just-bought stock at a higher price than you paid. This agreement money is paid to you right away, on the very next business day—money that's yours to keep forever. Your second source of profit could be the cash dividends due you as the owner of the stock. The third source of profit would be in the increase in price of the shares, from what you paid, to the agreed selling price.
>
> By agreeing to sell at a higher price than you bought, all you are giving up is the unknown, unknowable profit possibility above the agreed price. In return, for relinquishing some of the profit potential, you collect a handsome amount of cash that you can immediately spend or reinvest, as you choose. (p. 166)

Note the way Gross frames the cash flows into three "sources of profit" rather than integrating the three into an overall net cash flow. Of course, standard investors have no difficulty in integrating the cash flows, and they understand that covered calls provide no free lunch. But not all investors can disentangle the cash flows from their frame, and covered calls remain popular.

As Ross (1989) wrote, when standard finance scholars are asked to explain the proliferation of financial products and the features of their designs, they tend to "fall back on old canards such as spanning." Ross emphasized the role of marketing in the world of financial products. Shefrin and I (1993a) have shown that an understanding of the behavior of individuals and institutions explains the design of covered calls, money market funds, and many other securities.

## Behavioral Forces That Shape Financial Regulations

"Do you know what the concept of suitability means in the context of investments?" I ask financial economists. Few know, and few investment textbooks mention suitability. In contrast, suitability regulations are well known to securities brokers. Perhaps financial economists within standard finance ignore suitability regulations because they are not important, or perhaps they ignore them because suitability is difficult to fit into standard finance.

Suitability regulations revolve around the responsibilities of brokers to their customers. Brokers are required to ascertain that the securities they recommend are suitable for their customers based on the customers' financial conditions and needs. Consider the experience of Charles Schwab & Company. Charles Schwab is, of course, a discount broker that provides no investment advice. An investor was trading options through Schwab and lost $500,000. Then, claiming that those investments were unsuitable for his financial condition and needs, he sued Schwab. Schwab's argument in its defense was that it does not give advice; it merely trades what the investor wants traded. The arbitration panel said that Schwab's argument is irrelevant, the option trades were not suitable for that investor, and the fact that Schwab is a discount broker does not exempt it from suitability regulations.

The typical reaction of financial economists when they are told about suitability regulations is that these regulations are senseless and should be abolished. Suitability regulations prevent investors from using their investor sovereignty to choose the securities they want and construct the portfolios that are, in their judgments, optimal. The role of a theory is to explain the evidence, however, not argue with it.

Suitability regulations make no sense in standard finance because, in standard finance, people are assumed to be free of cognitive errors and problems of self-control. Suitability regulations are important, however, for behavioral investors. Indeed, suitability regulations can be understood as tools that help behavioral investors control the effects of their cognitive errors and self-control problems. In that sense, suitability regulations are analogous to "cooling-off" regulations.

Consider the door-to-door sales of vacuum cleaners. By law, a customer has three days after making a purchase, a cooling-off period, to cancel the transaction. The existence of this law implies that people have realized that sometimes they get too "hot" for their own good; they need time to cool off, think clearly, and regain their self-control. So, through the legislative process, people created a law that helps them control their cognitive errors and imperfect self-control. The same argument applies to securities. People understand that cognitive errors and imperfect self-control interfere with good decisions. So, through the law, they appoint a broker or investment advisor to do for them what parents do for children—say no to choices that parents judge irresponsible.

Or consider state merit, or blue-sky, regulations. Under them, a bureaucrat in, for example, Sacramento decides whether a particular security can or cannot be sold to residents of California. The rationale behind merit regulations is that people are susceptible to cognitive errors and, left to their own devices, will overpay for securities. As in the case of suitability regulations, merit regulations are designed to protect investors from themselves, protection that makes no sense in standard finance.

Consider merit regulations in light of the evidence on the returns from initial public offerings. Mounting evidence indicates that investors who buy IPOs in the public market, on average, lose substantially. Left to their own devices, IPO investors overpay for IPOs. Should merit regulations be abolished or, given the evidence on the returns IPOs provide, should the regulations be tightened?

Suitability and merit regulations are not the only tools designed to help behavioral investors cope with their shortcomings. Shefrin and I have analyzed suitability, merit, and such other regulations as those pertaining to insider trading and mandatory disclosure (Shefrin and Statman 1992, 1993b).

## Conclusion

Standard finance is well built on the arbitrage principles of Miller and Modigliani, the portfolio construction principles of Markowitz, and the CAPM of Lintner and Sharpe. Standard finance does not do well, however, as a descriptive theory of finance. Investors regularly overlook arbitrage opportunities, fail to use Markowitz's principles in constructing their portfolios, and fail to drive stock returns to levels commensurate with the CAPM.

People in standard finance are rational. They are not confused by frames, they are not affected by cognitive errors, they do not know the pain of regret, and they have no lapses of self-control. People in behavioral finance may not always be rational, but they are always normal. Normal people are often confused by frames, affected by cognitive errors, and know the pain of regret and the difficulty of self-control. I argue that behavioral finance is built on a better model of human behavior than standard finance and the better model allows it to deal effectively with many puzzles that plague standard finance, among them, the puzzles discussed here—investor preference for cash dividends, investor reluctance to realize losses, the determination of expected returns, the design of securities, and the nature of financial regulations.

Finance offers many other puzzles. Some are small—for example, why the practice of dollar-cost averaging persists despite its inconsistency with standard finance (Statman 1995). Some are large—for example, why investors ignore Markowitz's rules of portfolio construction (Shefrin and Statman 1995b). These puzzles might be solved within behavioral finance.

Financial professionals who understand behavioral finance will understand their own behavior and improve their decisions. Institutional investors who understand behavioral finance will understand the beliefs and motives of their clients and will be better at serving and educating them.

# Question and Answer Session

Meir Statman

**Question:** What is "quality of management," and how do we measure or quantify it?

**Statman:** Quality of management is the rating of quality of management by respondents to *Fortune's* survey of companies. Respondents give each company a score on quality of management ranging from zero (absolutely awful) to ten (glorious). The correlations cited in the presentation are based on the averages of those rankings from all the *Fortune* respondents. We do not know the respondents' thought processes in assigning the ratings.

**Question:** Did you examine the relationship between past stock performance and management ratings from the *Fortune* survey?

**Statman:** Yes, and the answer is in a paper that Roger Clarke and I wrote (Clarke and Statman 1994). One of the characteristics of high-quality companies is that their past stock returns are high.

**Question:** As a matter of communication, can we educate ourselves and our clients to look at portfolios rather than segments? If so, how?

**Statman:** It is possible to educate people, but we need more than education. I begin my talk about portfolios in my investments class by telling students that their intuition is likely to mislead them. What is really needed are structures that prevent us from acting on wrong intuition—for example, a work sheet with boxes that must be filled in—a framework that forces us to consider factors that, acting on intuition alone, we are likely to miss.

**Question:** With all the information available about the benefits of indexing—costs are low and managers have difficulty outperforming the indexes—why aren't more people indexing?

**Statman:** Indexing does not correspond to investors' intuition about the way the market works. I ask my students, "When you buy a stock because you are confident that it is a bargain, who do you think is the idiot who is on the other end of the transaction?" Most have never thought about this question. Most people do not think about the stock market as a zero-sum game relative to index funds. They do not consider the likelihood that the trader on the other side of the trade might be an insider and that they, in fact, are the patsy.

**Question:** Some of the findings of decision theory suggest that individuals overpay for volatility, whereas your research suggests that individuals overpay for stability, or good companies. How do we reconcile these views?

**Statman:** People frame their money into those different pockets. So, there is no unified attitude toward risk. Many people who buy insurance also buy lottery tickets. Are they risk averse or risk seeking? Investors divide their money into "safe" money and "risky" money (Shefrin and Statman 1995a).

**Question:** A so-called new finance is driven heavily by market inefficiency. Where does behavioral finance fit in this approach—as a subset or as the keystone?

**Statman:** Behavioral finance is a replacement for standard finance as a descriptive theory. The return anomalies are the pebbles in the shoe that make one say, "Enough! Standard finance does not work." When standard theories of portfolio selection are inconsistent with the evidence and when market forces are inconsistent with the predictions of the CAPM, the wise move is to go back to an examination of the financial decisions of individuals.

Moreover, the activities of individuals and institutions are a legitimate concern of the field of finance even if they do not affect prices. When corporations fail to deploy their assets efficiently, welfare declines. Agency theory focuses on the issues that pertain to welfare losses and mechanisms for alleviating such losses (see Jensen and Meckling 1976). Welfare losses also exist when individuals fail to construct efficient portfolios; a description of such losses and mechanisms for the alleviation of such losses are a concern of finance practitioners and should be a concern of finance academics.

As behavioral finance develops, we ought to keep in mind that we need theory that contains testable hypotheses, not stories. I take delight when somebody finds evidence contrary to hypotheses of behavioral finance. At least nobody can say that our theory is a just-so theory that cannot be refuted by evidence.

Moreover, explaining the existing anomalies is not enough. Behavioral finance will be tested in its ability to explain phenomena that are not even recognized today as anomalous within standard finance.

# The Principal–Agent Relationship and Investment Decision Making

Leslie Shaw
*President*
*Leslie Shaw and Associates*

Common reactions to the principal–agent relationship inherent in the investment industry structure may contribute to the poor performance of active managers. The idea that incentive fees will ameliorate this problem, however, is not supported in behavioral research. The suggestion here is that improved financial decision making must be grounded in the findings that decisions, rather than being based on maximizing some utility, are constructed on the spot by adaptive decision makers. Therefore, sponsors and managers should be considered joint problem solvers making decisions for their joint benefit.

The principal–agent relationship is a primary concept in economics, but little theoretical development or empirical work has been done on the relationship's importance in the money management business. This presentation begins with a focus on that sparse research. Next, select academic and practitioner attitudes toward the fee structure in the money management business are discussed, followed by an analysis of whether incentive fees are likely to improve principals' and agents' decisions in money management. Finally, the presentation addresses improving decision making by using the findings of behavioral research as well as agency theory.

## Research Findings

Few studies of the principal–agent relationship have been directed specifically to the domain of money management. Indeed, only three studies appeared from 1968 to 1989.

The most comprehensive study to date was written by Lakonishok, Shleifer, and Vishvy for The Brookings Institute in 1992. Its findings on money managers' performance simply corroborated previous findings, but the authors were the first to probe for the cause of poor manager performance within the principal–agent relationships existing in the industry. The substantial evidence presented in the study included the following:

- Active management subtracts value, regardless of investment style.
- Active trading among mutual funds does not produce superior performance; some evidence suggests that mutual funds are better than managers.
- Performance persistence among managers is remarkably lacking, but some evidence indicates consistency over three-year horizons. The more skillful managers outperformed other managers, but they did not outperform passive benchmarks.

The study suggests that agency issues are causal to poor performance in the following ways:

- The principal–agent relationship between a corporate office and a treasurer's office creates a bias against passive management because such management would reduce demand for the treasurer's services.
- The treasurer's office also has a bias against internal money management because external management allows flexibility and reduces the treasurer's responsibility.
- Corporate sponsors cannot perfectly observe the quality of money managers; therefore, the sponsor's task is not trivial. In carrying out that task, sponsors have a lot of information at their disposal, and they use it to allocate funds.
- But money managers also have some control—over the information that they reveal.

According to the authors, this structure leads to certain predictable responses from sponsors and managers. Sponsors have two basic responses. Some choose to index, although they still give the decisions regarding which index to use to an outsider. Some choose to diversify across styles, which can lead to a "closet index" approach.

Managers respond to the agency issues in the industry structure by designing strategies that give the appearance of product differentiation and by window-dressing their portfolios at critical times. Examples include the dumping of poor investment performers at the end of the year and/or the use of "lock-in" strategies (that is, when managers are ahead of their performance index they will switch to indexing in order to lock in the superior performance).

The authors concluded that much of the organization of the industry is driving managers' needs to provide sponsors with good excuses for poor performance, clear stories about strategies, and other services that are related only vaguely to performance. They predicted a trend ultimately toward greater rationality through more mutual-fund-style management and corporate use of defined-contribution plans in which individuals make decisions about their own fund allocations.

The Brookings study did not offer much encouragement to active managers. Yet there are many practitioners and a few academic consultants to the industry who believe improved performance will be derived from incentive fee structures.

## Fee Structure

Change in the fee structure of the industry has been recommended as a way to align the interests of sponsors and managers (see also Grinold and Rudd 1987 and Record and Tynan 1987). Academic consultants and industry practitioners have slightly different perspectives on this issue, but the evidence from behavioral research provides clear conclusions about the validity of incentive fees as causes of improved performance.

### The Perspective of Academic Consultants

Consultants to the industry promote incentive fees as a way to align sponsor and manager interests. Sponsors do not want passive management at the cost of an active fee, and although incentive fees do not entirely solve this problem, they are expected to influence the aggressiveness of many managers.

To address known deficiencies in practice, academic consultants suggest that a tailored incentive fee structure should include:

- Fairness. Fees should be a reward for skill.
- Coincidence of goals. The fees should assure the sponsor that the manager is acting in the best interest of the sponsor.
- Informativeness. The fee structure should tell the sponsor something about the manager's skill and the manager's confidence in his or her skill.
- Self-selection. Sponsors should tailor the fee structure so that the only managers who accept it will be those whom the sponsor would have chosen anyway.

Structured properly, incentive fees are supposed to help the sponsor split the managers into those who are confident of supplying exceptional return and those who are not. An improved fee structure should also induce the use of complex hedging strategies or portfolio insurance. It is further argued that tailored fees will be a causal factor in improving the validity of forecasting and the assumption of "appropriate" risk.

### Practitioner Perspective

Practitioner recommendations are similar to those of academics in many ways. Practitioners believe, first, that fees must be fair and reasonable no matter what the structure. Some practitioners have suggested, for example, that if there is an incentive fee, there should also be a penalty. And because much information about fee structures in the industry is readily available, comparison benchmarks can be determined for proper evaluation by manager and sponsor. Second, practitioners say that fees should be clearly understood, especially in the case of complex fees. The implication is that managers should be prepared to explain their decision processes to sponsors and sponsors, in turn, should be allowed the opportunity to conduct analyses of the managers' processes. Third, fees should not pose an unacceptable conflict; they must be in the interest of the client and must not cause the manager to behave so as to benefit only the manager.

### The Evidence about Incentives

These recommendations from professionals within (or close to) the industry are all based on a belief that incentive fees play a major role in judgment accuracy and subsequent financial achievement. The basic model is one of "effort for accuracy." The conventional wisdom is that decision strategies should pursue maximum accuracy and that incentives can be structured to elicit and reward the expanded effort and accuracy in manager judgments.

Unfortunately, this overall approach is a fallible one. More than a decade of behavioral research on the effects of incentives provides substantial evidence to their detriment within the effort/accuracy model. An overview of the evidence about incentives is as follows:

- Incentives do not work by magic. They work

by focusing attention and by prolonging deliberation. Therefore, incentives are more likely to prevent errors that may arise from insufficient attention and effort than they are to prevent errors that arise from misperception or from faulty intuition.

- A substantial part of the incentive philosophy among industry professionals, as noted, is that "appropriate" incentives could/should build judgment confidence. The detriment, however, is that incentives more often lead to the phenomenon of overconfidence in judgment and a deterioration in performance. An important question at issue here is: Why does decision-maker confidence necessarily have any measurable correlation with consistent accuracy? The evidence says it does not.
- Devoting more effort to the use of a flawed decision strategy—if it is, indeed, a flawed strategy—will only worsen performance.
- The size of the incentive can be thought of as analogous to the speed with which one travels in a given direction, but it is cognition that determines the direction to be traveled. If incentives are high but cognition is faulty, one simply gets to the wrong place faster.

Thus, all professionals—sponsors and managers alike—should be wary of the frequent claim that the failures of rational thinking result from the costs of the thinking process and that such failures can be eliminated by proper incentives. In order for incentives to change decisions or strategies and increase performance, a manager must believe that his or her current strategy is insufficient in terms of desired accuracy. After all, if managers do not think a current decision process is broken, they are not likely to fix it. For incentives to lead to a strategy shift, a better strategy must be available; if the manager does not know what to do, higher incentives for "doing it right" will probably simply cause panic. Finally, people must believe themselves capable of executing the new, hopefully better, strategy.

## An Exercise in Decision Making over Time

In order to capture a working idea of the elements in making judgments over time, imagine that you have been hired to manage a machine that produces widgets. Your job is to make decisions about the control state of the machine's process by monitoring each observation of output. Based on experience, you know that the machine is working correctly when the overall process produces observations that fall between 80 and 120 on a time-series screen. **Figure 1** shows 21 observations of the widget production process when it is working properly.

**Figure 1. Record of Widget Production Quality When Machine Is Working**

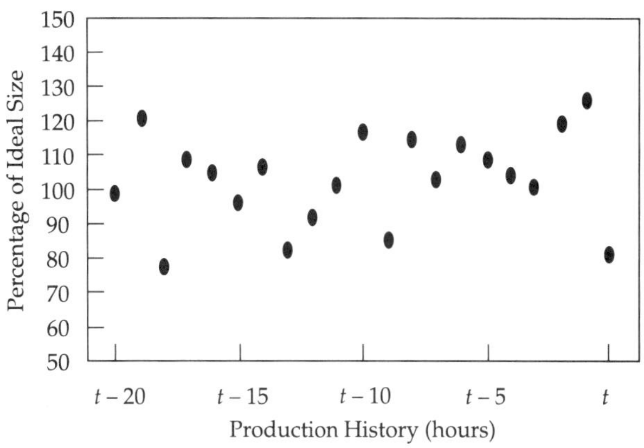


*Note*: *t* = total observation period.
*Source*: Leslie Shaw and Associates.

Periodically, the machine goes out of control, which shows up in high and low marks on the quality record, but then readjusts within the "working" range. And sometimes, the entire process goes out of control, in which case, the machine is broken and must be turned off for repairs. If it breaks on the high side, the report of the out-of-control machine looks as it does in **Figure 2**. If it becomes out of control on the low side, it looks like **Figure 3**.

**Figure 2. Record of Widget Production Quality When Machine Is 20 Percent Too High**

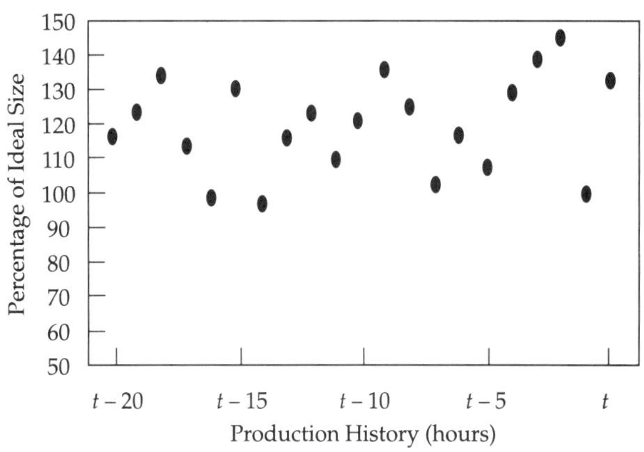


*Source*: Leslie Shaw and Associates.

Your job is to determine whether your machine is working or broken. You will be paid through the following incentive scheme: As you watch each observation appear, you must decide whether the machine is working or broken. If you believe the machine is working and you are correct, you will gain a point. If you believe it is not working and you are wrong, you will lose a point. If you believe the ma-

**Figure 3. Record of Widget Production Quality When Machine Is 20 Percent Too Low**

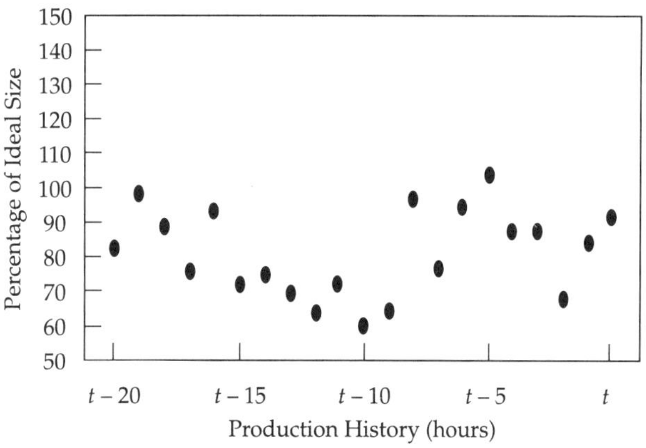


*Source*: Leslie Shaw and Associates.

**Figure 4. Widget Machine after Five Observations**

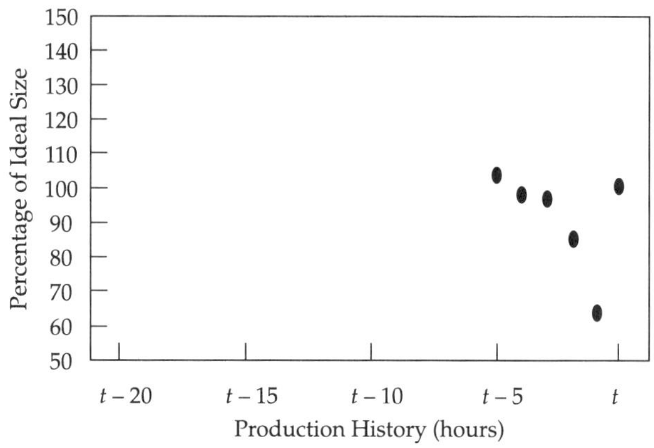


*Source*: Leslie Shaw and Associates.

chine is broken, you must shut it down for repairs. If your judgment is correct, you will gain a point. But if you shut the machine down because you think it is broken and you are wrong, you will lose a point. In summary, your incentive scheme is

| | Action | |
|---|---|---|
| Reality | Fix Machine | Leave Alone |
| Machine is working | –1 | +1 |
| Machine is broken | +1 | –1 |

Therefore, noticing when the machine is, in fact, broken really pays off, but you do not want to shut it down if you do not have to. On the other hand, the longer you wait to fix the machine if it is broken, the more you will lose, because the process accumulates if the machine continues in a broken state.

No doubt, you see the analogy here to portfolio management. How long do you hold the stock, in your belief that the earnings process is working, before you make a decision that the stock should be sold? And what are the costs of making the wrong decision to sell a stock that appears to have moved into a state of long-term losses when, in fact, a short series of performance downturns do not indicate a poor long-term performer?

Returning to the imaginary task, **Figure 4** presents a machine that has produced only six observations. Do you believe that it is working or broken? **Figure 5** and **Figure 6** show machines that have broken at various stages in the process. Try putting your hand on the page and uncovering each observation one at a time. Would you have determined a working or broken machine correctly each time the process actually broke and shifted to a different state?

When this task has been carried out by many decision makers, each of whom has begun with a new machine and made decisions in 500 trials, the results provide several conclusions. First, the overwhelming tendency for participants is to shut down the machine (bail out of the process) far more often than is optimal. Second, variations in the reference point of the observations determine whether the outcome is perceived as a gain or loss. Participants think that the working state remains more often than is the case. Third, participants evidently do not learn from experience. When participants are told whether their judgment of a broken process was correct or not, even with (especially with) feedback about how well they are doing, their performance diminishes greatly. Fourth, if a short-term trend, up or down, occurs in the picture of observations, the ratio of working to broken judgments drops from 15:1 to 7:1. The ratio of correct to incorrect judgments, however, remains at 2:1 regardless of whether there is an upward trend to the data, a downward trend, or no trend at all. The implication is that when trends appear, people believe something is happening to the process and they react to it, but they are not sure how these observations should affect their judgments about the working order of the machine.

**Figure 5. Widget Machine Breaks Low at *t* – 10**

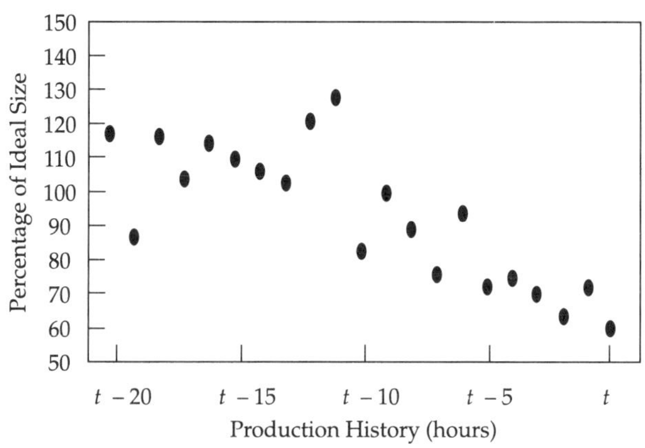


*Source*: Leslie Shaw and Associates.

**Figure 6. Widget Machine Breaks High at $t-2$**

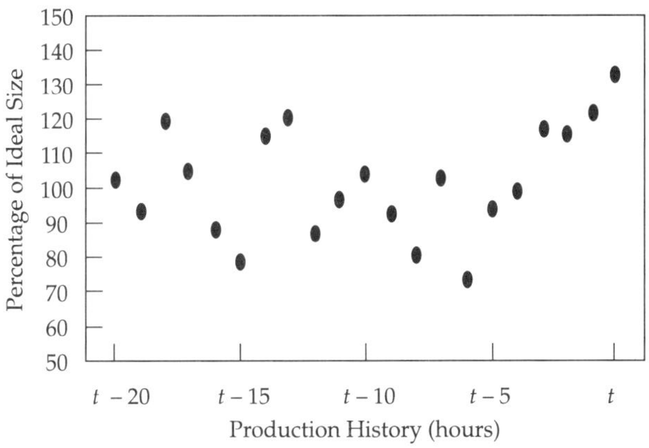


*Source*: Leslie Shaw and Associates.

## Improving the Overall Decision Process

The broken/working machine task provides some lessons that may be applied to the portfolio management process.[1] First, some learning from investment management experience and from previous strategies does occur, but the learning does not occur *because of* incentives. Also, learning the "right lessons" from investment choices will occur only under certain conditions; such learning requires an accurate and more immediate feedback than is the norm in the investment environment. Moreover, important financial decisions are often made in unique circumstances, which offers little opportunity for learning.

The past two decades of research in behavioral economics has led to a conception of choice that is different from the idea of a complete preference order for all options and a preference order from which the "best choice" is always selected. In other words, behavioral research is revealing that "maximizing" choice is probably not possible. We now believe that preferences for choice—including, of course, financial decisions—are constructed on the spot by adaptive decision makers. The normative prescription that individuals should maximize some quantity may be wrong.

So, the sponsor–manager relationship in the money management industry can be considered a constructive process. A basic tenet of economics is, after all, that the joint gains from trade arise from the differences between the parties. The two must simultaneously discover and exploit their differences. Even simple arrangements between principals and agents carry many information and incentive burdens—for example, "risk perception," "risk preference," and the chosen "allocation of risk." Perhaps *nothing* exists to be maximized! The ordering of choices, especially in complex financial decisions, can be only partial because the calculations are impossible in principle. Therefore, because the principal–agent relationship has so many different, incommensurable goals to achieve and because financial preferences are so labile and readily manipulable, perhaps principals and agents should be considered joint problem solvers, not maximizers.

Money managers' and clients' interests should be not only to understand financial decision making but to improve it, and the truth (about improvement) ultimately resides in the process, not in the outcome. The practice task was intended to be a simple example of this truth. When principals and agents are viewed as problem solvers, the opportunity to manage financial decisions for their joint benefit arises. Such a constructive approach to the process may help market analysts develop rationales for action; justifications other than the short-term utilities of the sponsors and managers could be equally legitimate, if they are thoughtfully derived.

### The Basic Approach

Decision outcomes can be used to define a model of a good decision process. Even though good decisions may sometimes lead to bad outcomes because of uncertainty, the basic approach is that *good decision-making processes tend (on average) to lead to more desirable outcomes than do poor decision-making processes.* Imagine, then, that within the principal–agent process, a model of a good process that is unique to manager–sponsor needs could be derived in this way: by comparing many decisions that result in positive and negative outcomes and by then identifying the systematic differences between those processes. This approach is offered as an alternative to the normative, rational standards that investment professionals have traditionally been trained to pursue.

The true potential value of this alternative, however, is related to the following issue. Suppose researchers in recent years had somehow demonstrated that whereas people's decisions may not lead to the outcomes they had forecast with the frequency they would like, nonetheless their choices did conform to the standards of rationality and the internal consistency that is the normative standard of expected utility. Would researchers then conclude that people are making the best possible decisions for themselves? Would they conclude that principal–agent decisions in this industry are the best for the decision makers? Would such a finding imply that the outcomes of people's decisions are desirable? Based on the records of performance published in the Brookings paper and other sources, the answer is probably no. Even if people conform to the measur-

[1]The framework and recommended alternatives that follow come from recent publications by psychological researcher Paul Slovic (1995) and from Deborah Frisch and Robert T. Clemen (forthcoming) at the University of Oregon.

able criteria of expected utility and rationality, they may be doing a poor job of specifying the uncertainties they face and/or the consequences of their actions. Perhaps, therefore, even expected-utility maximizers can improve their overall decision processes.

In fact, some researchers now claim that a person who maximizes decision utility is not necessarily maximizing "experience utility." Therefore, a recommended perspective on the decision process is: A standard of decision making should provide guidelines about *how* one should make decisions in order to balance the desirability of outcomes against the chances of obtaining them.

How can an alternative standard of a good decision-making process be developed and justified? Recent research in behavioral decision making suggests that three basic features are necessary for good decision making. First, it should be based on the relevant consequences of different options (consequentialism). Second, it should be based on an accurate assessment of the world and a consideration of relevant consequences (thorough structuring). Third, the process should contain trade-offs of some form (a compensatory decision rule).

▪ *Consequentialism*. In order to achieve a balance between desirability and likelihood of outcomes, decision processes should focus explicitly on the consequences of different outcomes that may occur. For example, is the financial decision actually based on a consideration of the desirability and likelihood of outcomes rather than on other, nonconsequential arguments, such as habit or corporate tradition? Is the decision consistent with the desirability of the outcomes?

The validity of strategies that include consequential thinking can be tested with certain questions: Are managers more satisfied with the decision outcomes when they have included the use of consequentialist strategies? Are good outcomes often associated with consequentialist strategies and bad outcomes associated with nonconsequential strategies?

▪ *Thorough structuring*. Thinking about consequences is not sufficient; structuring is also needed. Structuring is the process of identifying the possible actions one might take, identifying different consequences of the actions, and assessing the likelihood and desirability of those consequences. How many options do managers typically generate in making a decision? Are certain classes of consequences, such as long-term consequences, systematically ignored? Are certain consequences, such as short-term emotional consequences, overweighted? To what extent are surprising or unexpected consequences of a decision the result of a failure to predict accurately what will happen versus a failure to predict accurately how one will experience the consequence?

▪ *Compensatory rule*. When decisions may have several different consequences, decision makers should attempt to make trade-offs among them. Why? Because the decisions are more likely to achieve desirable outcomes if they reflect all possible consequences of actions.

### Benefits of the Alternative Framework for Decisions

Nothing in the preceding suggestions contradicts the old notions of expected utility; in fact, the two perspectives overlap. Utility theory was developed at a time when psychological research was grounded in behaviorism; the new framework says that decision makers will benefit from a normative standard that is based more on realistic cognitive processes than behaviorism. The justification for any standard of good decision making must be its reliance on the empirical findings that identify the aspects of the decision-making processes that lead to desirable outcomes. The derivation of and understanding of optimal rules serve both principal and agent if the rules include the outcome standard that resides within the processes, because the *truth* is in the decision process.

## Conclusion

The principal–agent relationship in money management has been compared to sharecropping. The agent is the farmer in the field putting in the effort, the principal is the landowner, and the sharing of the money made is an example of a fundamental information problem in the face of risk (such as rain/no rain). So, a rule is needed for deciding how much money the landlord should keep and how much should be given to the farmer. To solve the problem, one needs to know such things as whether the output is a function of skill or luck; that is, if the output is small, is bad luck the reason (such as bad weather) or was the farmer lazy?

In the money management business, quantitative economists would set this problem up as an infinite period problem: Based on this year, determine the next requirement. So, they would ask what kinds of rules money managers are working under now. What are sponsors telling managers? Given the ability of the agent, what rules can be acceptable to sponsor and manager together?

In "The Loser's Game" (*Financial Analysts Journal*, 1975), Charles Ellis provided some specific guidelines for rules of the investment management game. I paraphrase them here and relate them to the lessons of this presentation.

- Know your policies well and play according

to them all the time. In the widget machine task, the biggest winners are the managers who stick to their decision policy regardless of short-term feedback.

- Play the shot you have the greatest chance of playing well. Simplicity, concentration, and economy of time and effort have been the distinguishing features of the great players' methods. In other words, think about consequences and spend your time and effort on thorough structuring of the problem.
- Concentrate on your defenses. The competition in making purchase decisions is too good, so concentrate on selling instead. In the widget machine task, the biggest losers are always those who do not concentrate well on when to shut the machine down, get out of the process.
- Efforts to beat the market are no longer the most important part of the solution; they are the most important part of the problem. So, perhaps the compensatory trade-off part of the process is the key to improved performance solutions for today.

## Question and Answer Session

Leslie Shaw

**Question:** You alluded to the fact that mutual funds' performance may be better than that of investment advisors dealing directly with their clients. Is there some reason to believe that the less managers communicate directly with clients, the better their performance will be?

**Shaw:** That is the conclusion in the Brookings paper; it is not necessarily mine. Not talking to clients would be only a short-term solution. The long-term consequences of such an action are still a question. The issue is like the good news/bad news routine:

If you talk less, you might be less affected by immediate feedback from the sponsor that leads to knee-jerk reactions, but talking less may have a long-term negative impact on the total relationship, which also contributes to performance.

**Question:** Managers always claim that they can do better than the benchmark against which they will be measured—often, 4–6 percent better. Sponsors know they cannot, that they are trying to get the business, but how can a plan sponsor deal with that problem of overconfidence in the manager community?

**Shaw:** In terms of the recommended alternative framework for decisions, some joint acceptance of a "base rate of error" over the long haul will diminish the need for short-term performance targets that feed the overconfidence syndrome. Getting the decision rules out on the table is vital.

**Question:** When you are asked by a firm to study their decision-making process, what are the key questions you ask?

**Shaw:** There is only one key question: What is the decision rule you are using? The rest of the firm's actions evolve from that question.

# Behavioral Biases and Alphas

Russell J. Fuller, CFA
*President*
*RJF Asset Management Inc.*

Alphas have two sources—unique information or the ability to exploit somebody else's behavioral bias. The research reported here explored the relationship of low and high predictability (past forecast errors of earnings per share) to investor returns. Surprisingly, high-predictability stocks provided higher returns with substantially less risk than low-predictability stocks. The explanation may lie in a behavioral bias: Analysts seriously overestimate the next year's earnings for low-predictability companies.

As the presentations in this proceedings reveal, investment decisions are strongly influenced by people's behavior. This presentation first discusses the conflict between the assumptions of classical economic theory and perceived market behavior. It then describes the findings of a study on the returns of low- and high-predictability companies that suggest behavioral biases at work in some market anomalies and, therefore, in generating alphas.

## Behavior and Economic Theory

All economic theories rest on explicit assumptions about markets and on some behavioral assumptions, either explicit or implicit. One behavioral assumption is that people act in their own self-interest. This assumption is not always true, however. For example, suppose you are visiting Los Angeles and you go to a restaurant. You do not expect ever to come back to this restaurant. Would you leave a tip? I suspect you would. Leaving a tip under such circumstances is not in your economic self-interest, however; so forces other than self-interest must be at work.

The second assumption is that investors are economically rational, that in setting prices, investors act in an economically rational way to maximize the expected value of their portfolios. This assumption also is not always true. For example, under this assumption, stock returns should not be influenced by the weather, but a 1993 study by Edward Saunders found evidence that they are. Hypothesizing that people are optimistic on sunny days and depressed on rainy days, Saunders classified each trading day in New York City as sunny if it had 0–20 percent cloud cover and rainy if it had 100 percent cloud cover. **Table 1** compares the daily mean percentage change in three indexes for two time periods from 1927 through 1989. Although the differences between daily returns and weather are small in magnitude (and probably not economically exploitable), they are highly significant in a statistical sense. This finding suggests that so-called rational factors are not the only determinants of prices. Why would sunshine affect stock prices other than for purely behavioral reasons?

In addition to the assumption that investors are rational, the efficient market hypothesis assumes that they use all known information to set prices in ways that maximize the value of their portfolios. The implications of this hypothesis are well known: All known information is reflected in the price; thus, *ex ante* (expected) alphas are zero and active management is not worth the cost; *ex post*, however, alphas can be quite different from zero because of new information that causes prices to change.

In such a framework, the only sources of alpha are unique information or insights and behavioral biases. Most active managers attempt to generate positive alphas through their unique information or insights. If no unique information is available, then the only way to generate a positive alpha is to find situations in which the known information is not properly reflected in the price. In these cases, the question is *why* the information is not reflected in the price. The answer must be that the players are either maximizing something other than the value of their portfolios—something else in their utility function that has priority, such as a behavioral issue or an agency conflict—or they are making some sort of cognitive error in using the known information.

**Table 1. Mean Percentage Daily Index Change**

| Time Period | Sunny | Cloudy | Difference |
|---|---|---|---|
| 1927–62 | 0.032% | –0.016% | 0.048% |
| 1962–89 | 0.065 | –0.028 | 0.093 |

*Note*: 1962 data break at July 4–5. Daily index change represents the average of five indexes: the DJIA, the capitalization-weighted NYSE and Amex, and the equally weighted NYSE and Amex.

*Source*: Saunders (1993).

The information associated with the documented anomalies in the investment literature—such as the low-P/E or small-firm effects—is widely available. Three possible explanations have been put forth to explain anomalies. First, because of measurement errors, methodological errors, or the studies being time specific, the results are purely spurious. Second, the risk–return model is misspecified; in other words, for something to be called abnormal, it must be compared with what is normal, but the true risk–return model is not known. In this case, the anomalies may not be actual anomalies but, instead, may be correlated with factors the model is not taking into account. Third, the anomalies are caused by behavioral biases. Thus, in competitive markets, the only sources of "true" mispricing (the chance for positive alphas), given the known information set, are behavioral biases.

## Predictability Bias

Lex Huberts and I conducted a study of "predictability bias," which we believe is a behaviorally induced anomaly (Huberts and Fuller 1995). The study was designed to determine whether low-predictability or high-predictability companies have, in the past, provided investors in U.S. stocks with the higher returns. The measure of predictability was the three-year average absolute value of past forecast errors of earnings per share. Companies were classified into two groups based on how hard or easy predicting their earnings had been in the past three years: low predictability for hard to predict, and high predictability for relatively easy to predict.

Typically, low-predictability companies are small and have low price-to-book ratios (P/Bs) and high betas. Because low P/B is supposed to be associated with high returns, people tend to believe low-predictability companies have generated higher returns. The study found, however, that high-predictability stocks provided higher returns with substantially less risk than low-predictability stocks. **Table 2** shows year-by-year returns for industry-diversified predictability quintiles, and the results are consistent across the time period. In fact, the differential return is negative for 10 of the 11 years.

We concluded that we might have found a persistent market anomaly. But for investors to exploit a persistent anomaly, they must know the story behind it—the economic and behavioral factors that are driving it. Otherwise, if the story could not be determined, the anomaly could be spurious—that is, the product of noise or random chance. Therefore, we began a search for the reasons behind the findings.

The anomalous-looking results had several possible explanations. We had examined low levels of risk and P/Bs and found no correlation with the results; we also examined other well-documented anomalies, such as P/E. Eventually, we concluded that the driving force behind this result is a behavioral bias: Analysts seriously overestimate the next year's earnings for low-predictability companies.

The empirical implication of this hypothesis is that low-predictability companies will probably have large negative earnings surprises. If, during the first part of the year, analysts seriously overestimate the earnings of low-predictability companies, then as the year progresses, either analysts will revise their estimates downward or the companies will subsequently report earnings that are well below the estimates (i.e., negative earnings surprises). Consequently, nobody would want to own the low-predictability companies.

To investigate the idea of negative surprises, after we ranked these companies on the absolute value of the forecast errors, we looked at the signs of the forecast errors for the coming year. As **Table 3** shows, on average, the forecasts for low-predictability companies were too high by 23.5 percent, compared with only 2.5 percent for the high-predictability companies. As in Table 2, the results in Table 3 are quite consistent from year to year.

Although we did not construct a rigorous test of why analysts miss their forecasts, we can speculate on the explanation as follows. First, for many reasons, we observe substantially more buy recommendations than sell recommendations. For one thing, brokers and sell-side analysts have incentives to produce buy recommendations. Also, on average, there is a net inflow of money into the capital markets; thus, the demand by investors for purchase recommendations exceeds the demand for sell recommendations. In addition, most active managers do not engage in short selling, which limits the size of an active bet against an overpriced stock to the stock's weight in the benchmark. In contrast, infinitely large bets can be made by purchasing underpriced stocks. Also, investment banking relationships may provide disincentives for analysts at underwriting firms to issue sell recommendations. Analysts may not want to jeopardize their relationships with corporate officers, who are a prime source of information for analysts. Finally, a sell recommendation may carry a "relationship cost" for analysts who have previously recom-

**Table 2. Median Total Returns for Industry-Diversified Predictability Quintiles**

| Formation Date of Quintile | Return Period | Predictability Quintiles Q1[a] | Q2 | Q3 | Q4 | Q5[b] | Difference (Q1 – Q5) | t-Statistic |
|---|---|---|---|---|---|---|---|---|
| *Holding period T1* | | | | | | | | |
| 4/80 | 5/80–4/81 | 39.1% | 42.4% | 41.9% | 39.0% | 42.1% | –3.0 | –0.8 |
| 4/81 | 5/81–4/82 | –12.8 | –12.8 | –8.7 | –8.0 | –8.9 | –3.9 | –1.5 |
| 4/82 | 5/82–4/83 | 52.5 | 47.8 | 44.3 | 44.9 | 49.5 | 3.0 | 1.3 |
| 4/83 | 5/83–4/84 | –0.1 | 1.0 | 3.9 | 0.0 | 1.5 | –1.6 | –0.4 |
| 4/84 | 5/84–4/85 | 5.8 | 13.1 | 24.0 | 21.7 | 27.8 | –22.0 | –5.1* |
| 4/85 | 5/85–4/86 | 23.4 | 31.4 | 39.0 | 40.7 | 36.7 | –13.3 | –3.9* |
| 4/86 | 5/86–4/87 | 8.7 | 9.9 | 10.7 | 14.8 | 16.6 | –7.9 | –4.3* |
| 4/87 | 5/87–4/88 | –9.8 | –7.3 | –2.4 | –3.6 | –2.1 | –7.7 | –3.2* |
| 4/88 | 5/88–4/89 | 14.6 | 14.4 | 14.8 | 16.3 | 15.6 | –1.0 | –0.5 |
| 4/89 | 5/89–4/90 | –7.5 | –1.7 | 3.9 | 7.5 | 8.4 | –15.9 | –5.2* |
| 4/90 | 5/90–4/91 | 0.0 | 6.8 | 8.8 | 13.9 | 14.8 | –14.8 | –4.8* |
| Average for T1 | | 10.4 | 13.2 | 16.4 | 17.0 | 18.4 | –8.0 | –3.8* |
| *Holding periods T2 through T4* | | | | | | | | |
| Average for T2 | | 8.4 | 10.7 | 13.1 | 14.4 | 15.9 | –7.5 | –3.8* |
| Average for T3 | | 11.5 | 14.7 | 15.2 | 15.9 | 18.3 | –6.8 | –5.6* |
| Average for T4 | | 9.3 | 11.2 | 11.6 | 12.7 | 13.6 | –4.4 | –2.9* |
| *Risk-adjusted abnormal returns, holding periods T1 through T4* | | | | | | | | |
| Average for T1 | | –8.2 | –5.1 | –0.8 | 0.5 | 2.2 | –10.4 | –4.4* |
| Average for T2 | | –7.8 | –5.8 | –2.3 | –0.7 | 0.7 | –8.5 | –4.4* |
| Average for T3 | | –7.4 | –2.8 | –2.8 | –0.9 | 0.8 | –8.2 | –7.0* |
| Average for T4 | | –6.6 | –3.5 | –2.8 | –2.1 | –0.8 | –5.8 | –3.6* |

*Note*: Risk-adjusted returns are computed as the individual security return minus its beta times the return on the market. Betas are estimated using five years of historical returns and the S&P 500 Index as the proxy for the market portfolio.

[a]Lowest predictability.
[b]Highest predictability.
*Indicates statistical significance at the 1 percent level.

*Source:* Huberts and Fuller (1995).

mended purchase at higher prices.

A second explanation for why analysts miss their forecasts may be that portfolio managers are much more likely to act on an analyst's buy recommendation with a big earnings number attached to it than one with a small earnings number attached to it.

Third, the less predictable the earnings have been in the past, the more difficulty the portfolio manager will have seeing an optimistic bias in the earnings forecast, if there is one. In contrast, if the company's

**Table 3. Median Signed Forecast Errors for Industry-Diversified Predictability Quintiles**

| Forecast Error Period | Q1[a] | Q2 | Q3 | Q4 | Q5[b] | Difference (Q1 – Q5) |
|---|---|---|---|---|---|---|
| 1980 | 3.2% | 3.8% | –0.5% | 0.9% | 0.0% | 3.2% |
| 1981 | 12.8 | 9.0 | 2.3 | 1.5 | 0.6 | 12.2 |
| 1982 | 33.3 | 22.4 | 21.7 | 11.1 | 9.0 | 24.3 |
| 1983 | 8.4 | 9.0 | 3.8 | 1.1 | 1.6 | 6.8 |
| 1984 | 20.8 | 8.0 | 3.1 | 2.9 | 0.7 | 20.1 |
| 1985 | 36.3 | 25.1 | 10.0 | 5.2 | 5.6 | 30.7 |
| 1986 | 45.7 | 18.3 | 9.2 | 5.4 | 2.9 | 42.8 |
| 1987 | 17.5 | 7.1 | 3.4 | 1.5 | 1.1 | 16.4 |
| 1988 | 20.6 | 5.8 | 2.3 | –0.2 | 0.0 | 20.6 |
| 1989 | 26.6 | 12.7 | 5.5 | 3.7 | 2.2 | 24.4 |
| 1990 | 33.0 | 20.0 | 14.3 | 5.5 | 3.6 | 29.4 |
| Average | 23.5 | 12.8 | 6.8 | 3.5 | 2.5 | 21.0 |

[a]Lowest predictability.
[b]Highest predictability.

*Source*: Huberts and Fuller (1995).

earnings have been fairly predictable in the past, imparting a significantly optimistic bias to a forecast is very difficult. Consequently, if analysts do have excessive optimism built into their forecasts, the bias is much more likely to be in the forecasts for companies whose earnings have been hard to predict in the past.

Overly optimistic estimates may be one reflection of overconfidence—if the low-predictability companies have a disproportionate number of turnaround situations, for example. Nobody has a clue whether such companies are, in fact, going to turn around. Overconfident analysts may think they have those situations figured out, so they come up with a big optimistic forecast. On average, however, the stocks for turnaround companies as a whole exhibit no earnings changes.

## Conclusion

Predictability bias is an example of an anomaly that is related to behavior—the systematic forecast errors of analysts. Such behavioral biases are a way of thinking about alphas. Alphas have two sources—unique information or the ability to exploit somebody else's behavioral bias.

In the past 30 years, the integration of classical economics with what used to be traditional financial analysis created modern finance. The major developments include the efficient market hypothesis, capital structure theory, portfolio theory, the capital asset pricing model, the arbitrage pricing model, and option-pricing theory. During the next 30 years, modern finance will be integrated with the behavioral sciences, and the result will be equally important.

# Question and Answer Session

Russell J. Fuller, CFA

**Question:** Can you describe the characteristics of the stocks in the study with regard to such traits as P/E?

**Fuller:** The study was designed to be industry neutral. For example, Quintile 1 represents the 20 percent of every industry that was the hardest to predict and Quintile 5 represents the 20 percent that was the easiest to predict, so no industry effect should occur. Q1 stocks have high betas, low P/Bs, and low yields, which makes sense. Managers of companies whose earnings are hard to predict are going to set lower payout ratios than those whose earnings are easy to predict.

Most of the characteristics increase or decrease monotonically as you go from Q1 to Q5. For example, P/B and beta increase systematically across quintiles from low to high in terms of past predictability. Yield is the exception; yield is low for Q1 but higher and about the same for the other four quintiles.

**Question:** Your test ended just before small-capitalization stocks moved strongly. Would the small-cap movement have affected your results if you carried the test into 1994?

**Fuller:** The results for predictability appear to be fairly consistent, although not always strong. Low-predictability stocks tend to be small companies, however, and in 1992 and 1993, low-predictability stocks seem to have performed better than high-predictability stocks. But if you adjust for size, they performed poorly. I hope someone does replicate the study for the recent period, but if the results are not to be confusing, they must control for such things as size and P/B effects.

This study covered a very short time period. You can always argue that anomalous results are simply time-period specific. The time period of the study is the only period for which we have reasonably good estimate data. We did create a proxy for predictability bias that went back into the early 1970s—the actual variance of earnings per share—and we found results that are roughly consistent with the findings reported here.

**Question:** A number of explanations of the Monday and year-end effects have been offered. Has behavioral finance made an attempt to explain these effects?

**Fuller:** Recent research shows that the small-cap effect at the end of the year is largely spurious, so in that case, there do not appear to be any behavioral issues. An interesting aspect with respect to small size and the year end, however, is this notion of marginal firms and seasonal effects. First, firms that are distressed are marginal—that is, have lots of debt or low equity relative to debt, and so forth. Distressed firms benefit when the economy picks up, and they benefit more than nondistressed firms. Second, seasonality does occur in industrial production; the economy does tend to pick up in December and January. So, the seasonal boost may account for part of the year-end effect and a lot of the general small-firm effect.

I am not aware of any good explanations for the Monday effect. Why returns are low on Monday relative to other days of the week is a mystery. It must rain a lot on Mondays.

# Behavioral Biases and Investment Research

Richard S. Pzena
*Director, U.S. Equity Investments*
*Sanford C. Bernstein & Company, Inc.*

The strategy of investing in companies with low price-to-book ratios continues to be successful in the long term. Historical evidence on reversion to the mean justifies the strategy, but it is seldom consistently pursued because environmental pressures on investment analysts make the strategy almost unbearable to maintain. To counteract the pressures and focus analysts on the low-P/B strategy, investment firms need to focus on analyzing the long-term expectations for companies, not short-term stock price forecasts, and avoid intuitive, emotional investment decisions.

Analysts have biases because, contrary to popular wisdom, they are human beings and, therefore, are affected by the same emotions that affect all human beings. They despise uncertainty. They orient their behavior to avoid anxiety and to seek out the warm, fuzzy feelings that come from success. They will do almost anything to achieve those kinds of feelings. They are also influenced by the press, their peers, their bosses, and their clients, all of whom unknowingly encourage them to be emotional creatures. To eliminate the emotions that cause these biases is impossible; the best that can be done is to try and tone them down a little. Fortunately, analysts do not have to eliminate their emotions; simply limiting the emotions' influence will make the difference between good and mediocre investment performance.

The focus of this presentation is the tension between the forces that lead to superior long-term investing and the environmental influences that affect research analysts—that is, the pressures that create biases—and the effects of those biases. The presentation will suggest some ways to structure research and investment practices and procedures to tune out the biases.

## Price-to-Book Ratio

Consider first a very basic dynamic—one that underlies all of investment history: In a nutshell, it is that buying stocks with low price-to-book-value ratios works. **Table 1** shows the performance of the lowest P/B quintile of the S&P 500 Index against performance of the full index for successive five-year periods since 1970. In virtually every period, simply buying the 20 percent of the index with the lowest P/Bs produced excess returns.

Why does this anomaly persist? A low-P/B strategy is simple, does not cost much, and works. What prevents analysts from following this approach? The answer is discernible in the following simple list of P/B Ratios as of March 1995:

| | |
|---|---|
| Cray Research | 0.5 |
| Chase Manhattan | 0.9 |
| Kmart | 1.0 |

These are the low-P/B companies that the strategy requires one to buy today. But what images come to mind when people think about Kmart? Chances are they picture an old, rundown company with 1950-style stores, out-of-stock shelves, and discourteous employees. Most people prefer to shop at Wal-Mart, because Wal-Mart has great prices, always stocks what they need, and has friendly employees and clean stores. Analysts have the same thoughts and emotions.

As an alternative to Kmart, the low-P/B investor might decide to buy Cray Research. Cray sells for half of book value. But what images does it bring to mind? Cray makes supercomputers in a world where personal computers are up to almost any task. What about Chase Manhattan Bank? It has a knack for lending money to people who cannot repay it.

Now, compare these companies with the following high-P/B list, stocks the low-P/B investor must *not* buy:

| | |
|---|---|
| Coca-Cola | 12.7 |
| Microsoft | 8.3 |
| U.S. Health Care | 7.7 |

History suggests that investing in companies like

**Table 1. Performance of Low-P/B Stocks**

| Years | Low P/B | S&P 500 | Premium |
|---|---|---|---|
| 1970–74 | 4.5% | –0.4% | 4.9% |
| 1975–79 | 28.5 | 14.8 | 13.7 |
| 1980–84 | 23.6 | 14.8 | 8.8 |
| 1985–89 | 20.5 | 20.4 | 0.1 |
| 1990–95[a] | 12.8 | 9.9 | 2.9 |

[a]Data for 1995 are through February.

*Source*: Sanford C. Bernstein & Co.

these is a losing strategy. They are just too good. Their stellar records, however, permit investors to sleep well at night. People associate them with growth, stability, innovation, and good management, and investors are willing to pay a premium for those characteristics. They will accept lower returns in order to avoid the stress and anxiety associated with companies on the other list.

Not many investors want to go to a cocktail party and explain why they own Kmart. They will accept the lower return of Coca-Cola in order to avoid that explanation—and headlines like "Kmart chief under siege, resigns post"; "Kmart to shut 110 stores, eliminate 7,000 jobs"; "Wal-Mart soars while Kmart sags"; "Sale at Kmart: damaged goods." And it is not the analyst alone who reads these portents. So do all his or her peers, bosses, and clients.

Even the experts run away. PaineWebber will not touch the stock: "The hole Kmart has dug for itself is large." Lehman Brothers says, "Kmart still has a long road ahead, and we expect it to remain bumpy." Wertheim Schroder doubts the company has a sales strategy and recommends selling. Goldman, Sachs diplomatically observes that "management has a stiff challenge to restore the company's luster." The investor who goes against all this advice suffers sorely.

The analyst also confronts the historical data shown in **Table 2**. Kmart sales are falling; profit

**Table 2. Kmart Financial Data**

| Financials | 1992 | 1993 | 1994 |
|---|---|---|---|
| Sales (billions) | $37.9 | $34.4 | $34.9 |
| Operating margin | 4.4% | 3.1% | 1.8% |
| Debt/total capital | 55.0 | 63.0 | 68.0[a] |

[a]End of third quarter.

*Source*: Sanford C. Bernstein & Co.

margins have collapsed; debt is rising. And what has been happening to Wall Street earnings estimates? Progressive deterioration, as shown in **Figure 1**. Deep down, the analyst knows that buying low-P/B stocks makes sense, but recommending Kmart requires courage.

The high-P/B list is a much more pleasant world. The headlines are all positive: "Microsoft marches

**Figure 1. Kmart Consensus Earnings Forecast**

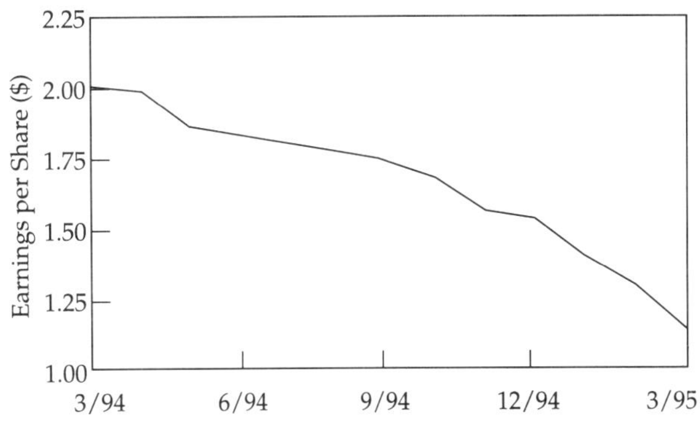


*Source*: Sanford C. Bernstein & Co.

into Asia"; "Bill Gates *Financial Times* man of the year"; "Warp speed needed to catch Microsoft"; "Microsoft has online services quivering." The analyst receives additional good news from the financial fundamentals, as shown in **Table 3**. Sales are grow-

**Table 3. Microsoft Financial Data**

| Financials | 1992 | 1993 | 1994 |
|---|---|---|---|
| Sales (billions) | $2.8 | $3.8 | $4.6 |
| Operating margin | 36.1% | 35.3% | 37.1% |
| Debt/total capital | 0.0 | 0.0 | 0.0 |

*Source*: Sanford C. Bernstein & Co.

ing more than 20 percent a year; profit margins are stable to increasing; the company has no debt at all. The consensus earnings expectations are stable, as shown in **Figure 2**. Anyone who recommends this stock can sleep well at night.

**Figure 2. Microsoft Consensus Earnings Forecasts**

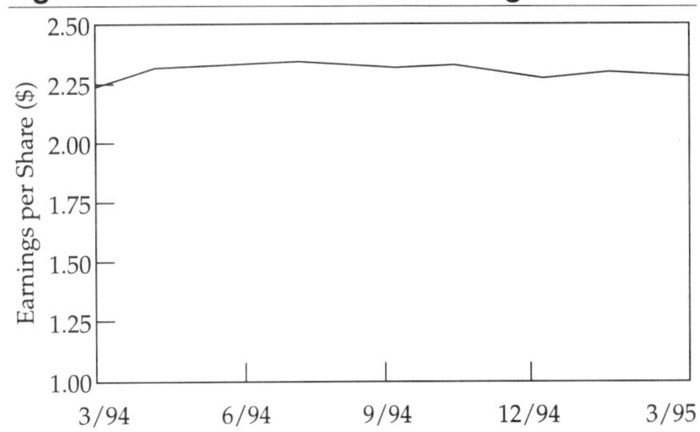


*Source*: Sanford C. Bernstein & Co.

So, people tend to buy Microsoft and avoid Kmart even though history shows that, in the absence of other information, Kmart is the better investment. The investor who bought all the Kmarts of the world and avoided all the Microsofts of the world would win.

## Reversion to the Mean

Stocks become cheap because of a progressive deterioration that eventually leads to surrender: The stock's price collapses to book value or below. How, then, can a low-P/B investor win? Why does investing in these deteriorating companies make sense?

The reason lies in reversion to the mean. **Figure 3** illustrates how this phenomenon manifests in the business world. Essentially, bad companies get better, and good companies deteriorate. Figure 3 shows the S&P 500 for the last 20 years divided into quintiles based on each company's return on equity (ROE). The lines show the quintiles' performances during the following five years. The Q1 line represents the least profitable companies in a base year and traces their succeeding five-year performance. Basically, Q1 companies are making no money and have zero ROE in the base year. Figure 3 shows that they have 10 percent ROEs five years later. Of course, some companies *do not* turn around and end up bankrupt; the line shown is the average for the group, including the failures. In contrast to Q1, the most profitable companies in the base year—the Q5 line—begin with ROE of 25 percent and end at 15 percent.

**Figure 3. Reversion to the Mean by S&P 500 Quintiles**

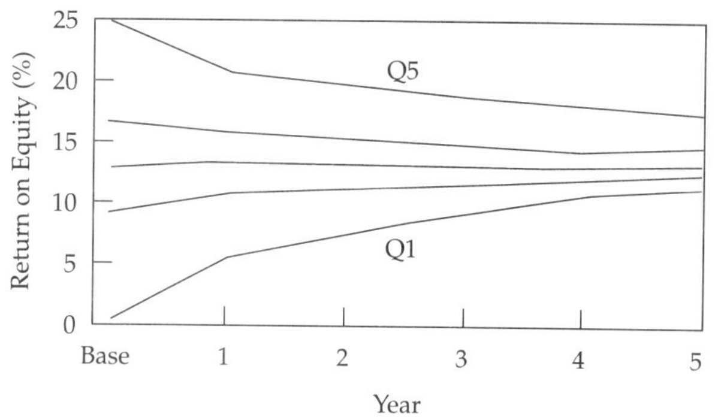


*Source*: Sanford C. Bernstein & Co.

Why do these reversions occur? The answer is human nature. Those who have the misfortune to be managers of Q1 companies do not usually say, "This is a lousy company. I quit." They are more likely to try and do something: cut costs, close inefficient capacity, introduce new products, change the management team. Managers of Q5 companies have very different problems. Everybody in the world wants part of their business, so the managers spend most of their time fending off competitors that want to emulate the successful strategy and get a piece of the pie. No matter how hard the managers resist, history shows that those competitors *will* get a piece of it. The evidence is compelling that competition will arise. The successful company's growth rate will slow, and its profit margins will fall.

Q1 represents the companies with low P/Bs. The odds are in favor of the investor who buys these companies, even if a few of them go bankrupt. The odds are very much against those who buy the Q5 companies—not that such investors cannot win, but they can win only if they happen to pick the companies that do not revert to the mean. The Q1 investors are swimming with the current. In behavioral terms, Q1 investors are getting paid to take the anxiety that Q5 investors refuse to take.

Make no mistake: Q1 investing is painful. Anyone who inquires about Kmart's strategy will learn that its new management team is cutting costs, changing the merchandising strategy, and improving distribution. All the analysts that recommend selling Kmart know this story, but they do not believe it. They have good reason to doubt, but the odds are against them.

The implications of reversion to the mean for 1995 and 1996 consensus earnings forecasts for Kmart and Microsoft are in **Table 4**. Kmart is at $1.10 for 1995 and $1.30 for 1996. Analysts who believe in reversion to the mean and think Kmart's new management will succeed should forecast normal earnings power for Kmart by 1997—the point at which all the reforms take effect—in other words, earnings of $1.85. Less enthusiastic analysts, who believe Kmart will revert only to its subpar historical earnings level, should forecast $1.75. The fact is, however, that no analysts are forecasting $1.75 or higher for Kmart in 1997.

**Table 4. What Reversion to the Mean Implies**

| Share Data | Kmart | Microsoft |
|---|---|---|
| Price | $12.00 | $70.00 |
| Analyst earnings forecasts | | |
| 1995 | 1.10 | 2.30 |
| 1996 | 1.30 | 2.85 |
| 1997 forecast assuming: | | |
| Reversion to mean | 1.85 | 1.25 |
| Reversion to history | 1.75 | 3.00 |
| Price/normal earnings | 7× | 23× |

*Source*: Sanford C. Bernstein & Co.

Contrast the Kmart forecasts with those for Microsoft, which is expected to earn $2.30 in 1995 and $2.85 in 1996. If Microsoft reverts to the mean, it will earn $1.25 in 1997. If it can maintain its current profitability, it will earn $3.00. No analyst has 1997 earnings forecasts of less than $3.00 for Microsoft.

Which is the better investment? An investor can buy Kmart for 7 times normal earnings or Microsoft for 23 times $3.00 or 50 times the reversion earnings of $1.25. That difference is the opportunity investors obtain in buying the Kmarts of the world.

You may be thinking, "Reversion to the mean is a nice theory, but how does it work out for a low-P/B company in reality." The Kmart of 1990 is the Chrysler of yesteryear. Of course, now that Chrysler is the hottest car company in North America, people have trouble picturing it in the same league as Kmart, but as shown in **Figure 4**, Chrysler was probably in worse

**Figure 4. Chrysler: A Classic Cyclical, 1989–93**

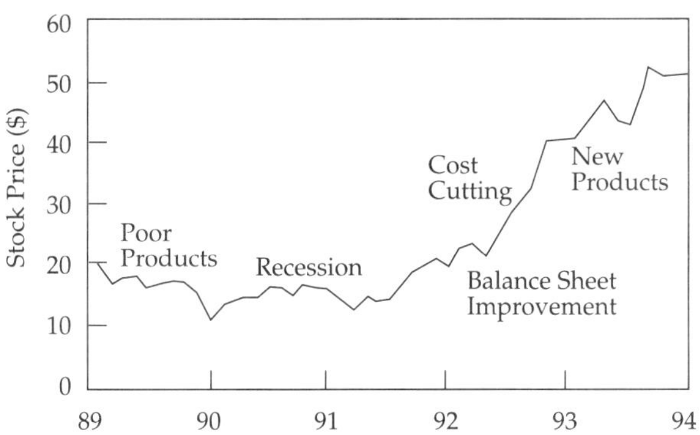


*Source*: Sanford C. Bernstein & Co.

shape in 1990 than Kmart is today. It had lousy products, high costs, an uncompetitive design lead time, and during a recession, life-threatening debt. Chrysler's stock reflected these flaws; it dropped to $10 in 1990 against a book value of $21 and stayed there through 1991. The normal earnings per share, using reversion to the mean, was $5.

But the recession eventually ended, and Chrysler changed its products, copied Japanese car manufacturers by introducing products quickly, and improved its balance sheet. The stock rose to almost $60 in late 1993 and is currently producing $10 a share in earnings. This rags-to-riches story is repeated over and over again in the market for low-P/B companies. Not every story has a happy ending; sometimes problems take a very long time to resolve. But the phenomenon endures.

## How to Avoid Research Biases

Clearly, low-P/B practitioners must have high confidence in themselves and their systems. Sometimes they will feel very lonely. Everyone—their clients, their peers, the press—will question their sanity. Such pressure keeps their ranks thin, but because the rewards for following the low-P/B approach are significant, money managers and research firms need to structure their organizations so as to prevent analysts from succumbing to that constant pressure. Firms cannot eliminate the biases that result from the pressure, but they can tone them down.

At Sanford C. Bernstein, we have developed certain procedures to help prevent our analysts and investment policy groups from succumbing to bias. First and foremost, we have a systematic process to prevent making investment decisions on intuition or gut feeling. We follow two principles: We focus on the long term, and we separate forecasting from investing.

- *Focusing on the long term.* Many people make near-term earnings forecasts, but focusing on the short term merely exaggerates the biases caused by peer and market pressures. The first thing we do is ask our analysts to think long term. If asked to provide near-term earnings estimates, analysts will be biased by what is happening at the moment. Our analysts have one goal: to estimate a company's long-term, normal earnings level over a full economic cycle under the company's current strategies. All judgment focuses on the soundness of that forecast. Once satisfied with it, we compare it with the price of the stock.

- *Separating forecasting from investment decision making.* Many people pay analysts for their stock picks, but we pay them for their ability to make earnings forecasts. We ask them to forget about the stock and focus instead on how much money the company will make. In our investment committee meetings, we talk about companies, not stocks. We grill the analysts on long-term earnings expectations; we do not talk about current conditions or whether the timing is right.

This policy is our second line of defense against emotional decision making. Anyone who pays for stock picking gets the same thing everyone else has: opinions that agree with the emotions and the biases in the market. The difficulty of following such a policy is the difficulty of designing a system that rewards analysts on a long-term basis.

Among the characteristics we require of analysts is an explicit logic for ignoring reversion to the mean. We train analysts to find reasons companies making a lot of money cannot continue to make that much money.

They also need to be skilled at listening to the turnaround plans of the corporate managers and judging when a plan makes sense. We train our analysts to be skeptical. This function is difficult because analysts want to add value; they want to believe the managers will fix the companies. Avoiding companies that will not revert to the mean is critically important, however, so we train analysts to differentiate between a simple plan to deal with temporary, easy-to-fix problems and improvements that depend on fundamental changes in the world. Such changes rarely occur.

Finally, we total all our analysts' estimates and make sure the total makes sense. If current consensus expectations for the next couple of years were tracked and totaled, they would probably not make sense; they would likely describe an economy growing at something like 15 percent a year and profit margins and returns on investment at higher levels than ever seen in corporate U.S. history. If we find our totals are way out of line, we know that some company earnings forecasts are wrong and must be adjusted.

## Conclusion

The low-P/B approach is not easy. If you choose it, your forecasts will be out of line with everyone else's. You may be branded as a lunatic. If it leads to superior performance, however, lunacy may be better than what is branded at the outset as sanity.

# Question and Answer Session

Richard S. Pzena

**Question:** You could have bought Kmart a year or two ago, so why buy it now? What makes the timing right in terms of your systematic process?

**Pzena:** We did buy it a year ago. The biggest risk of this sort of investment approach is the timing risk; as the figures in this presentation indicate, three years or more pass, on average, before you see any improvement in one of these companies. A lot of pain can result from buying too early.

We approach the decision by waiting on the sidelines while Wall Street analysts are cutting their earnings estimates. Once they stop falling, we buy the stock. We followed that discipline with Kmart, but its earnings expectations stabilized and then resumed their deterioration. Now, they are stabilizing again, so now would be a better time to buy than a year ago. Now, you can go in and say it is cheap.

**Question:** How important is diversification in this approach?

**Pzena:** Diversification is an issue. When companies become cheap, a lot of their industry peers usually become cheap at the same time because the problems are not always company specific. Kmart's situation may be company specific, but the problems of banks, for example, are not; they are all facing the same issues. Our solution is simple:

If we have a big opportunity, we concentrate; if we have a modest opportunity, we diversify. If the low-P/B stocks in an industry are selling at 50 percent off fair value, you want to buy a lot of them. If the stocks are selling at 20 percent off, you do not want to be so exposed to one industry.

In 1990, low-P/B stocks, not only financials but cyclicals as well, were 50 percent off. We bought a lot of them. The portfolio was concentrated because we were getting paid to take on the risks of being concentrated. Today, we are paid much less to take on the risks of being concentrated, so we don't. Today, big opportunities are not available for this type of approach, and diversification makes sense—broad diversification across industries and across different types of risk factors.

**Question:** How do you know when to get out? Do the momentum players help you when these stocks turn?

**Pzena:** When earnings expectations are deteriorating, you should wait. When earnings expectations are rising, improvement occurs, which creates outperformance. When they stabilize and the stock has reached or exceeded fair value, you should get out.

# Exploiting Behavioral Finance: Portfolio Strategy and Construction

David N. Dreman
*Chairman and Chief Investment Officer*
*Dreman Value Management, L.P.*

Research shows that analysts' forecast errors are high. The findings reported here connect this outcome with behavioral tendencies toward extrapolation from the past, reliance on expert opinion and consensus, peer and institutional pressures, and extreme mispricing in the best and worst stocks prior to earnings surprises. Findings on reversion to the mean and behavioral factors may explain several market anomalies and the long-term success of contrarian strategies.

Analysts' estimates of company earnings form one of the cornerstones of all security analysis and are the bedrock of most financial theory. Earnings estimates require a fine precision, one that most practitioners believe can be obtained. Analysts aim to zero in on actual earnings—often, within 1–5 percent of actual earnings. When that goal is not reached, the result is sometimes enormous reaction in the stock price. In 1994, for example, Motorola reported earnings up 50 percent for the second quarter. These actual earnings were slightly less than 1 percent below the average analyst's forecast, however, and the stock dropped 15 percent in the next two to three months.

To the analysts' credit, they face a difficult environment, with thousands of inputs. Many decisions must be made about how to quantify a company's earnings estimates. A company may operate in as many as 50–100 different countries and have dozens of different products. Company managers, in doing their job properly, do not add to the precision. The analysts' job is difficult, and expecting them to estimate earnings on the nail every time is not realistic.

## Forecast Error

Analysts today have access to more information on which to base forecasts than ever before. Through First Call, for example, analysts can immediately obtain other people's or other analysts' changes of estimates. They have more online company financial data than ever. Nevertheless, forecast error rates seem to be rising—and rising significantly. **Figure 1** is from a study by Michael Berry and me (1995a) and shows analysts' forecasting errors as a percentage of reported earnings for 1,221 NYSE and Amex companies for all quarters between 1973 and 1990 For this study, we used consensus earnings estimates derived from the Abel Noser data base, the longest data base of quarterly earnings that we are aware of. The data base is composed of more than 1,000 large companies, with nearly complete coverage of the S&P 500 Index. Both current and delisted companies are included. At least six different analysts provided forecasts for each stock each quarter. For a major company, such as Microsoft, we may have had several dozen analysts' forecasts. Forecasts could be made at any time during the quarter, and both positive and negative earnings surprises were included. We had 66,000 consensus forecasts altogether, which would be at least 400,000 estimates.

The error rates are very high; annualizing the quarterly data, the average error was 42–43 percent. To assure that these results did not exaggerate the error rates, we screened out companies with small earnings, less than 40 cents a share annually. By doing so, we took out some of the fastest growing companies, of course, but the error rates were still high, about 22 percent.

Because forecasting must be very precise, the investment industry requires that money managers and analysts be able to fine-tune earnings estimates. We found, however, that 74.4 percent of analysts could not forecast within 5 percent of actual earnings, 57.0 percent could not hit within 10 percent of actual, and 45.3 percent were outside 15 percent of actual, a wide estimate range. Staying within a range of 10

**Figure 1. Forecast Error as a Percentage of Reported Earnings, 1973–90**

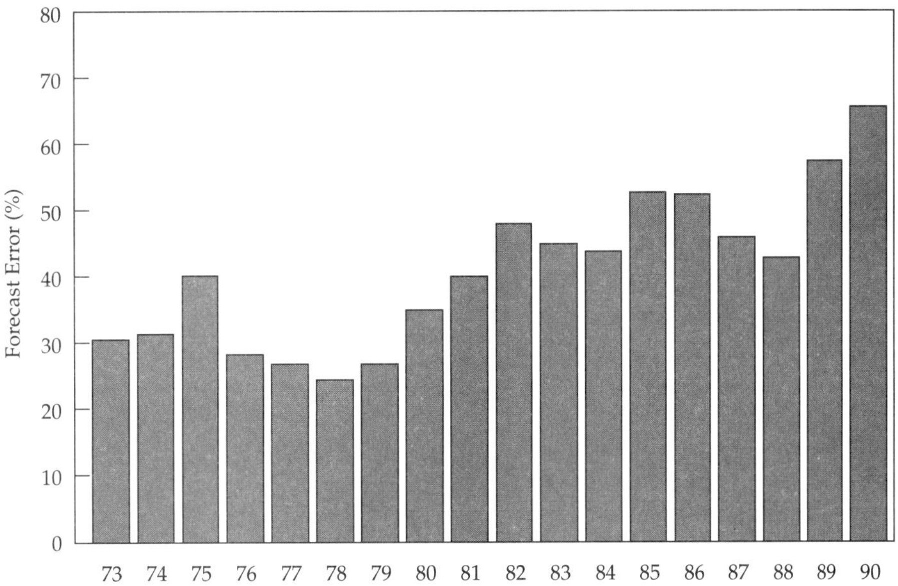


*Source*: Dreman and Berry (1995a).

percent is a reasonable expectation, and missing it is enough to trigger a stock reaction.

To make sure that the high overall forecast errors were not being caused by high forecast errors in only some industries, we performed the analysis again using 15 major industry categories. **Table 1** shows the error rate based on this analysis by industry groups. We found some volatility; forecast errors were actually much higher than expected in certain industries, especially those that are supposed to be reasonably predictable. For example, communications and consumer goods had 41 percent and 36 percent error rates, respectively. Tobacco was the only industry with fairly good stability. In all, the average error rate was 50 percent, and the median error rate was 43 percent.

**Table 1. Analysts Forecast Errors by Industry**

| Industry | Percentage of Annual Error |
|---|---|
| Capital goods | 55% |
| Chemicals | 28 |
| Communications | 41 |
| Consumer goods | 36 |
| Entertainment | 45 |
| Financial | 43 |
| Foods | 26 |
| Health care | 26 |
| Insurance | 33 |
| Metals/mining | 71 |
| Oil | 70 |
| Publishing | 27 |
| Textiles | 114 |
| Tobacco | 9 |
| Transportation | 75 |

*Source*: Dreman and Berry (1995a).

**Figure 2** shows the distributions of earnings surprises by four measures:

- SURPE: consensus earnings per share (EPS) surprise as a percentage of absolute value of actual EPS—that is, (Actual EPS – Forecast EPS)/Actual EPS.
- SURPF: consensus EPS surprise as a percentage of absolute value of forecast EPS—that is, (Actual EPS – Forecast EPS)/Forecast EPS.
- SURP8: consensus EPS surprise as a percentage of the past eight-quarter volatility of actual EPS—that is, (Actual EPS – Forecast EPS)/Standard deviation of trailing eight-quarter actual EPS.
- SURPC7: consensus EPS surprise as a percentage of the past seven-quarter volatility of change in actual EPS—that is, (Actual EPS – Forecast EPS)/Standard deviation of trailing seven-quarter change in EPS.

Four different surprise metrics were used because the academic literature lacks consensus as to the most appropriate form of the metric. Each measure has a unique set of statistical and interpretive problems, but our basic results were approximately the same for the four measures and consistent with earlier studies.

**Table 2** reports the results of forecasting error studies from the 1960s and 1970s. As shown, analysts are not the only ones who have problems forecasting; corporate managers do also. The first part of Table 2 reports findings on management forecasts, and the second part reports the findings of studies of ana-

**Figure 2. Distributions of Earnings Surprise Measures**

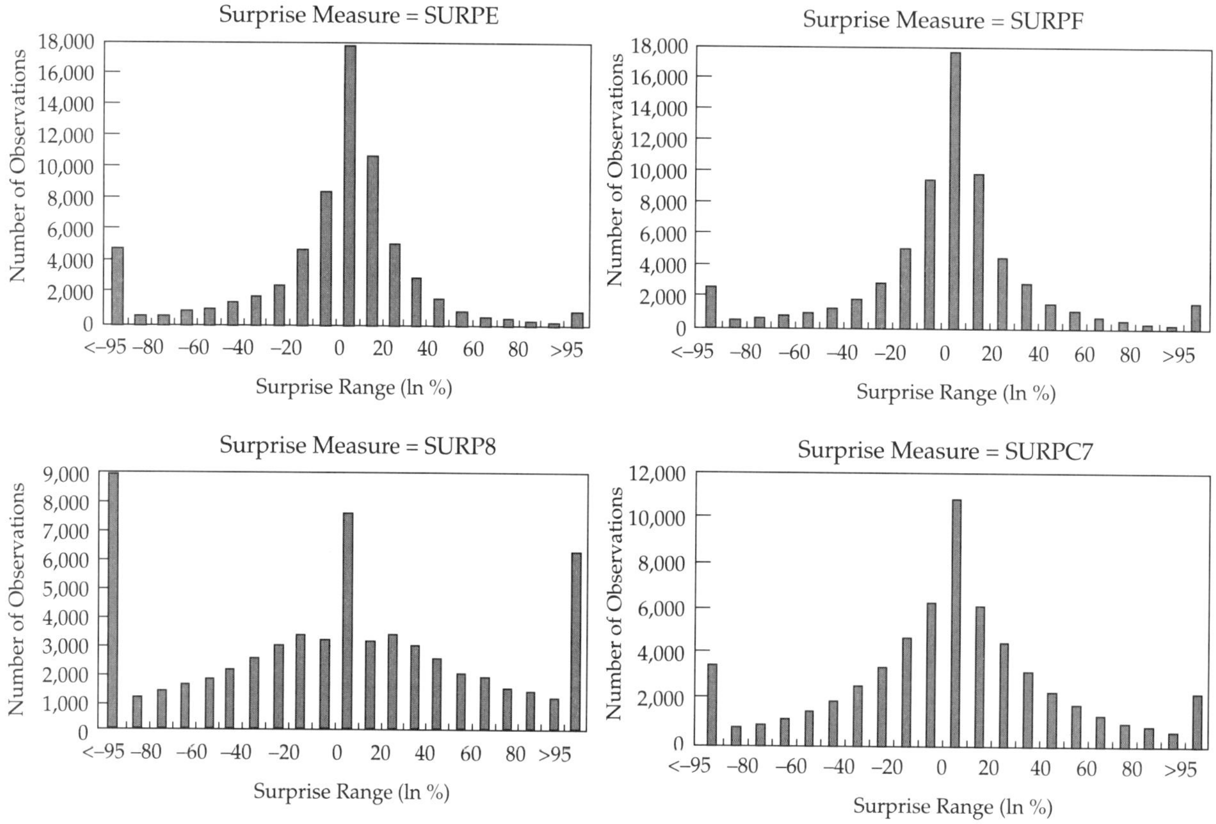


*Note*: All quarterly observations from first quarter 1974 through fourth quarter 1991.

*Source:* Dreman and Berry (1995a).

**Table 2. Findings of Forecast Studies: Managers and Analysts**

| Study | Period Studied | Number of Companies | Mean Error |
|---|---|---|---|
| | Management Forecasts | | |
| Green and Segall (1967) | 1963–64 | 7 | 14.0% |
| Copeland and Marioni (1972) | 1968 | 50 | 20.1 |
| McDonald (1973) | 1966–70 | 151 | 13.6 |
| Basi, Carey, and Twark (1976) | 1970–71 | 88 | 10.1 |
| Mean error | | | 14.5% |
| | Analysts' Estimates | | |
| Stewart (1973) | 1960–64 | 14 | 10–15% |
| Barefield and Cominsky (1975) | 1967–72 | 100 | 16.1 |
| Basi, Carey, and Twark (1976) | 1970–71 | 88 | 13.8 |
| Richards (1976) | 1972 | 93 | 8.8 |
| Richards and Fraser (1977) | 1973 | 213 | 22.7 |
| Richards, Benjamin, and Strawser (1977) | 1969–72 | 50 | 18.1 |
| Richards, Benjamin, and Strawser (1977) | 1972–76 | 92 | 24.1 |
| Mean error | | | 16.6% |

*Note*: Forecasts and estimates for one year or less.

*Source*: David N. Dreman.

lysts' forecast errors. The average error rate of managers forecasting for their own companies, usually in the first quarter, is about 14.5 percent. The analysts' error rate in these studies is about 16.6 percent.

## Reasons for High Forecasting Error Rates

The error rates found in our results and the results of some of the later studies are fairly similar, which suggests a number of interesting questions. First, what might be the reason for the high forecasting errors?

### Extrapolation

One reason, which has been demonstrated in the literature, is analysts' tendency to extrapolate past trends into the future. In the mid-1960s, Cragg and Malkiel (1968) carried out a study of analysts' estimates at six major buy-side investment organizations and a study of how the analysts carried out their research. They noted that, despite the fact that analysts did intensive and thorough research on companies, their estimates tended to be nothing more than extrapolations of past earnings.

Another interesting and relevant study, by Little and Raynor (1966), showed that no correlation exists between past earnings growth and future earnings growth for any three- or five-year period. Earnings follow a random walk. These results were disputed at the time, so Little redid the study—and came out with the same information. Later, Brealey studied 711 U.S. companies between 1945 and 1964. He also found that earnings tend to follow a random walk.

If earnings follow a random walk but analysts tend to extrapolate past earnings, the result should be fairly large forecast errors, which is precisely what the studies show.

### Behavioral Influences

Although earnings are almost impossible to fine-tune, most analysts and money managers place a great deal of emphasis on fine-tuned earnings estimates. In the first edition of *Security Analysis*, published in 1933, Graham and Dodd noted that the thorough analyst will go through hundreds and hundreds of factors—fundamental factors in a company and its industry, monetary conditions, and so forth—but in the end, the analyst will place the greatest emphasis on the short-term earnings forecast. Nothing much has changed since that study.

The behavioral questions are: Given the strong evidence that people cannot forecast in a precise manner, why is Wall Street so dependent on forecasting? Why is the Street so tremendously disappointed when earnings estimates are not met?

In 1984, Tversky and Kahneman published an excellent piece about how humans process information. They warned that cognitive biases affect the human processes of digesting and simplifying large amounts of complex information and that these biases can have major effects on decision making. Other cognitive researchers have aired similar findings. In 1982, Fischhoff warned that even when people are aware of their cognitive biases, they are not able to adjust for them. From a behavioral point of view, modification of analytical and decision-making methods is very difficult.

## Earnings Surprises and Investor Overreaction

The next issue is what actually happens when analysts' forecasts miss the mark. As mentioned in other presentations, investors appear to extrapolate exciting or unexciting prospects for stocks well into the future. The market has high expectations for the best stocks and very low expectations for stocks that are out of favor. Companies with the best prospects, fastest growth, and most exciting concepts normally have higher P/Es, higher ratios of price to book value and price to cash flow, and so forth. Sometimes, the disparity between valuations is enormous. Last year, for example, investors valued each dollar earned by General DataComm and Viacom at about ten times a dollar earned by Barnett Banks and the Federal National Mortgage Association, although Fannie Mae is probably growing at a 12 percent rate and has been for quite some time.

We have constructed and studied an investor overreaction hypothesis (IOH) to explain this phenomenon. The IOH posits that there is systematic mispricing of "best" and "worst" asset classes; that is, investors fairly consistently overvalue best stocks and undervalue worst stocks.

"Surprise" in these studies, which used the Abel Noser data base, was simply the analysts' forecast errors. A positive surprise was defined as any error above zero; any error below zero was a negative surprise. We made this simple rule rather than try to cut surprises arbitrarily at 10 percent, 15 percent, 20 percent, and so on. The best stocks in our classification were companies with the highest 20 percent of P/E ratios; the worst were companies in the lowest 20 percent.

The study of the IOH produced a number of findings:

- The study demonstrated an asymmetrical price reaction to earnings surprises for "best" and "worst" stocks. This hypothesis could apply to other contrarian valuation measures, such as price to book (P/B) or price to cash flow (P/CF).
- Favorable surprises for worst stocks raise

prices significantly over time, whereas prices for best stocks move down.

- Conversely, unfavorable surprises after the event quarter result in consistent above-average market performance for worst stocks and below-market returns for best stocks.
- The study also demonstrated postsurprise reversion toward the mean. Best stocks underperform and worst stocks outperform the market over five-year holding periods.
- Finally, positive and negative surprises have had little effect on the 60 percent of stocks grouped in the middle quintiles.

## Types of Earnings Surprises

In our study, Berry and I posited that the overreaction occurs before the actual earnings surprise, and we demonstrated that there are two types of earnings surprises: event triggers and reinforcing events. The event triggers and the reinforcing events result in stocks regressing toward the mean.

Event triggers cause changes in investor perceptions of best and worst stocks and result in large price movements. A positive surprise for an out-of-favor stock would be an event trigger; investors do not expect major good surprises for out-of-favor stocks. Similarly, for a stock very much in favor, a negative surprise would be an event trigger.

The other type of "surprise" is called a reinforcing event. Reinforcing events cause smaller market movements than triggers because they fit investors' current perceptions. An example would be positive news from a high-P/E or highly valued stock. People have favorable expectations for the best stocks—improved earnings and other positive events. Similarly, negative news for out-of-favor stocks should have little effect on stock price. If a company is trading at a very low P/E, P/B, or P/CF and is believed to have a mediocre outlook, a negative event is not likely to have a major effect.

Apple Computer's performance last year is an example of an event trigger—a positive surprise in an out-of-favor stock. Apple's Newton line of computers had been a failure, and many analysts thought Apple was losing market share in the personal computer business. When Apple introduced the PowerMac, revenues and earnings rose dramatically. The price of an Apple share more than doubled, from $22 to about $45.

The second type of event trigger is a negative surprise for a market favorite. For example, at the beginning of 1994, Biogen was at a very high P/E multiple, but after a number of disappointing quarters and other negative surprises, the stock dropped almost 50 percent.

Examples of two types of reinforcing events are Banc One and Duracell. Banc One, a low-P/E stock, had a minor problem in the fourth quarter of last year because of a write-off caused by derivatives losses in its portfolio. The stock dropped some, but within two or three months, it was higher than prior to the negative surprise. Duracell is a high-P/E stock and a major institutional favorite. Although earnings were above forecast in at least two quarters last year, the earnings surprises had very little impact on the stock price.

To summarize, according to our IOH, the net effect of surprises is positive for the lowest P/E quintile, but negative for the highest P/E quintile. The net effect is neutral for the middle quintiles.

## Impact of Earnings Surprises

The annualized impact of all earnings surprises for the entire period of our study is shown in **Table 3**. We used zero as the market or the sample average. The combination of all surprises, positive and negative, resulted in the low-P/E, most out-of-favor stocks having a 6.4 percent outperformance of the sample in the initial quarter in which the surprise occurred. The most in-favor stocks had a return of –5.0 percent in the initial quarter. Therefore, the difference between best and worst stocks, with all surprises, was roughly 1,100 basis points (bps). For the full year in which the surprise occurred in the first quarter, the out-of-favor stocks still had a 400 bp above-average market performance, an 800 bp difference in performance between best and worst stocks. By the end of the full year, the result was virtually no effect for the 60 percent of stocks in the middle quintiles.

**Table 3. Impact of Earnings Surprises on Performance: Annualized, 1973–90**

| Quintile | Quarter One | Year One |
|---|---|---|
| *All earnings surprises* | | |
| Lowest P/E | 6.42% | 4.13% |
| Middle P/E | –0.66 | –0.19 |
| Highest P/E | –5.01 | –4.21 |
| *Positive surprises* | | |
| Lowest P/E | 17.32 | 8.03 |
| Middle P/E | 10.98 | 3.77 |
| Highest P/E | 7.04 | 0.35 |
| *Negative surprises* | | |
| Lowest P/E | –4.43 | –0.88 |
| Middle P/E | –11.79 | –4.94 |
| Highest P/E | –18.40 | –9.55 |

*Source*: Dreman and Berry (1995b).

Table 3 also shows the impact of all positive surprises annualized. Positive surprises have an enormous above-market effect in the first quarter for the low-P/E stocks and much less effect on the best stocks. The annualized difference in the quarter is 1,000 bps, which holds up at 800 bps through the year.

The impact of negative surprises, the last set shown in Table 3, also indicates how dramatically different the effect of surprise is for best and worst stocks. The difference in reaction to surprise between worst stocks and best stocks in the first quarter is 1,400 bps. Even in a full year, the difference is enormous, almost 900 bps. Worst stocks totally absorb the surprise, and by the end of the full year, there is no impact on their stock prices.

**Table 4** shows the difference between impacts of the event triggers and reinforcing events. As expected, event triggers (the positive surprises for the low-P/E stock and the negative surprises for the high-P/E stock) have an enormous impact on prices.

**Table 4. Impact of Positive and Negative Event Triggers and Reinforcing Events**

| | Quarter One Annualized | | Year One | |
|---|---|---|---|---|
| Surprise | Low P/E | High P/E | Low P/E | High P/E |
| Event trigger | 17.32 | –18.40 | 8.03 | –9.55 |
| Reinforcing event | –4.43 | 7.04 | –0.88 | 0.36 |

*Source*: Dreman and Berry (1995b).

With the event trigger, the overall impact (total of absolute surprises) annualized for the quarter is almost 36 percent, and for the full year, the difference is about 17.6 percent. The reinforcing events (negative surprises for the low-P/E stocks and positive surprises for the high-P/E stocks) have much less impact. In the quarter, the total of absolute surprises is about 11.5 percent; for the year, 1.2 percent. All of these differences are statistically significant, and for some, the *t*-test would result in 1 in 10,000, 1 in 100,000, or higher.

**Figure 3** demonstrates the reversion to the mean for a 20-quarter period. Surprise has a major effect in the first quarter. The low-P/E stocks with positive surprises outperform the market in all 20 quarters. Moreover, the low-P/E stocks with negative surprises underperform only in the quarter of the surprise; then they outperform the market for the next 19 quarters. High-P/E reactions are exactly the opposite.

A summary of the return data is dramatic. For the low-P/E stocks that had a positive surprise, the absolute return in the quarter of the surprise was 4.29 percent above market and the overall five-year performance was 53.69 percent above market. The low-P/E stocks with negative surprises suffered a –0.49 percent effect in the quarter but outperformed the market for the full five years by 34.13 percent. High-P/E stocks with negative surprises underperformed the market by 4.98 percent on an absolute basis in the quarter and by a dramatic 56.04 percent for the five-

**Figure 3. Quarterly Returns for Positive and Negative Surprises**

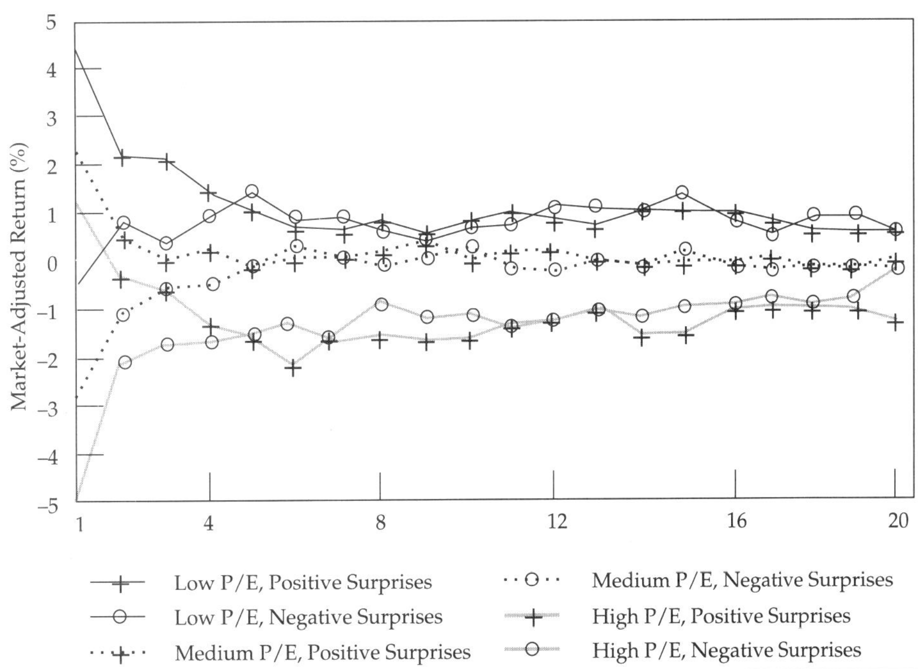


*Source*: Dreman and Berry (1995b).

year period. High-P/E stocks with positive surprises enjoyed only a 1.14 percent positive effect within the quarter, and for the holding period, they underperformed the market by 48.37 percent.

We believe this reversion to the mean results partly from the change in investor perceptions and partly because the surprise quarter is very likely followed by negative news for best stocks and by positive news for worst stocks. Note that surprise does not have much effect on the stocks in the middle; after the fourth quarter, they track the market.

Some research has shown that the growth rates of best and worst stocks—high- and low-P/E stocks—tend not to change much over some extended time period (Fuller, Huberts, and Levinson 1993). We found the difference in the price performance of the two groups, however, to be enormous. Even after 53 percent above-market return over five years, low-P/E stocks still had below-market multiples: The average for the quintile was 9.5 compared with roughly 12.5 for the market.

High-P/E stocks had above-market multiples—an average at the end of five years, even after their sharp underperformance, of about 15. These results support the part of the IOH that posits enormous mispricing of best/worst stocks prior to earnings surprises.

## Size and Frequency of Earnings Surprises

Finally, we wanted to make sure no other factors could have explained the results, so we examined two factors we thought were the most likely possible biases—size of earnings surprises and frequency of earnings surprises. Some researchers have recently proposed that high-P/E stocks have more negative surprises than low-P/E stocks. They also theorize that the sizes of negative earnings surprises are much larger for high- than for low-P/E stocks. We did not find either proposition to be true. **Table 5** contains the results for the size factor. With positive surprises,

**Table 5. Sizes of Earnings Surprises, 1973–90**

| Quintile | All Positive Surprises | All Negative Surprises |
|---|---|---|
| Lowest P/E | 17.45% | –79.46% |
| Middle P/E | 16.74 | –56.25 |
| Highest P/E | 22.08 | –81.25 |

*Note*: Percentage of actual.

*Source*: Dreman and Berry (1995b).

low-P/E stocks actually had an average surprise of about 17.5 percent, versus about 22.1 percent for the high-P/E group. High-P/E stocks had somewhat larger positive surprises and somewhat lower negative surprises, but results were not statistically significant.

Finally, we investigated whether a case could be made for the frequency of negative and positive surprises; for example, are negative surprises much more numerous for the best stocks than for the worst stocks. **Table 6** shows that the answer to this question is no. The differences are not statistically significant.

**Table 6. Number of Surprises, 1973–90**

| Quintile | All Positive Surprises | All Negative Surprises |
|---|---|---|
| Lowest P/E | 4,267 | 4,300 |
| Middle P/E | 12,046 | 12,924 |
| Highest P/E | 3,946 | 3,749 |

*Source*: Dreman and Berry (1995b).

We have checked other statistical factors but have found nothing that pointed to any factors other than simple stock mispricing prior to the measurement period to account for the effect of surprises.

## Conclusion

From the overall results, we have concluded that the returns from surprise are asymmetrical for best/worst stocks and that this effect is a result of extreme mispricing of the best/worst stocks prior to the occurrence of surprises. Surprises have little effect on the 60 percent of stocks in the middle. Event triggers—good news for the worst stocks and bad news for the best stocks—have much larger impacts on absolute prices than do reinforcing events—good news for the best stocks and bad news for the worst stocks. We have also shown that reversion to the mean begins in the first quarter following surprise and continues for each quarter throughout a five-year holding period.

We believe the explanation for these results is rooted in human behavior. As Amos Tversky discussed, the inability of money managers and analysts to estimate with precision is related to a natural tendency toward overconfidence.[1] Such overconfidence affects not only earnings estimates; it also affects judgments about which companies have excellent futures and which have very poor futures. We think a combination and interaction of factors are involved in the overconfidence—the reliance on expert opinion and consensus, for example, and peer and institutional pressures in the environment that push people toward favorite stocks and away from unfavored ones.

The reasons contrarian strategies work so well over time probably lie in behavioral factors. Contrarian strategies have been discussed for decades and

[1]See Professor Tversky's presentation, pp. 2–5.

have become even more appealing recently following the publication of Lakonishok's (1994) findings. Contrarian strategies are well documented and are not limited to pursuing low-P/E, low-P/B, or low-P/CF stocks. The average investor has difficulty sticking with a contrarian strategy. Researchers have the statistical results but have not pinpointed the behavior behind the statistics. Financial professionals are taught security analysis and the financial part of the equation, but the behavioral part is new territory.

We think the investor overreaction hypothesis probably applies to many other areas currently considered anomalies. Initial public offerings are a good example. Why do people consistently go into new issues when research shows that five-year returns on IPOs are slight to negative (Ritter 1991). Behavioral factors may also help explain returns on closed-end funds, junk bonds, and also the superior returns from financially distressed companies.

## Question and Answer Session

David N. Dreman

**Question:** Did the simple P/E-quintile split of your data base subject your results to industry bias?

**Dreman:** Probably, but only at times. For example, in 1990 during the financial crisis, about 75 percent of the stocks with low P/Es were financial stocks. On the other hand, if a strategy outperforms the market for decades, industry bias does not matter.

**Question:** Could seasonality be a factor?

**Dreman:** Seasonality is probably not a factor because we assembled new portfolios in each quarter.

**Question:** How do you explain the persistence of earnings surprises in terms of performance over such long periods of time as 20 quarters?

**Dreman:** We hope to finish a working paper on this question soon. We are finding that not only is overreaction an issue but so is underreaction. That is, economic theorists believe that markets should adjust immediately to all news, but in fact, markets do not adjust immediately to surprises. With the worst stocks, we found that only about 8 percent of the overall five-year return came in the surprise quarter. We believe a number of other surprises usually follow and that a perceptual behavioral change towards the company takes place only slowly. This change lasts much longer than three months; it goes on for at least five years.

Although we see an enormous first-quarter impact, it is only a small part of the total return. For example, if somebody, reacting to a negative surprise, were to sell a favored stock at the end of the surprise—three months after the first reaction—that person would still save most of the negative return. Similarly, with an out-of-favor stock, if somebody were to buy in the quarter after the positive surprise, that person would still get about 92 percent of the five-year return. The surprise quarter is the beginning of a perceptual change toward favored and unfavored stocks that lasts at least five years.

**Question:** Is the expectation of surprise cumulative or independent; in other words, if a company goes for a long time with steady earnings, is it building up for a surprise?

**Dreman:** When we look at these forecasts, the errors are so high that, statistically, over time—say, within a period of three to four years—the chance of surprise is high. Investors following a contrarian strategy know that the group of high-P/E stocks will contain any number of good companies but that, as a group, those stocks will underperform the market. As the study reported here shows, surprise works against favored companies. For contrarians, the choice is like going to a roulette wheel that has more reds than blacks: If you play the game long enough, the probability is that if you keep betting on red on that wheel, you will win.

**Question:** If everybody knows a stock is cheap, is it really cheap?

**Dreman:** What I have discovered in the last 20 years is that although the low-P/E effect is very well known, most people simply do not follow it with any consistency. Contrarian strategies ought to have far more practitioners than they have. I think they do not because these strategies do not work all the time. For example, low-P/E stocks underperform in some years. From the mid-1980s until 1987 and again in 1990 and 1991, low-P/E strategies underperformed. On the practical side, investors wonder if all the past trends have changed: "Is the world different now?" It is an unpopular strategy and difficult to stick with for the long haul.

**Question:** Do you believe that this particular way of looking at security pricing could be applied to closed-end country funds?

**Dreman:** Definitely. Closed-end funds are usually sold when enthusiasm is very, very high. Some of you might remember that after Spain entered the European Community, everybody believed Spain would be an enormous growth country. When the Spain Fund became public, it sold at about 150 percent of net asset value (NAV), although an investor could buy the same stocks *at* asset value. Then, in 1989, the Spanish government instituted a tight monetary policy, and by 1992, the country's growth rate had dropped to 1 percent. Today, the fund shares sell at about a 10 percent discount to NAV.

Such a development is not at all unusual for the country funds. The Latin America funds, for example, sold initially at enormous premiums. With the reunification of Germany in 1990, the German Fund went to a tremendous premium—approximately 200 percent—because investors believed

Germany was going to be the leading industrial country in Europe and have trade ties with eastern Europe. Reunification has, of course, caused Germany a lot of problems—recessions and so forth—and the fund shares have dropped sharply. This process occurs repeatedly with closed-end funds.

**Question:** Do you believe overreaction is the result of the investment industry's very short investment horizon?

**Dreman:** Definitely. Some findings of cognitive psychology strongly suggest that the recency and saliency of events have an enormous impact on investors. For example, if I buy a stock and the stock rises even though it was already at 40–60 times earnings, that good short-term experience may distract me from the fact that the probability is low that such a rise will continue for a longer period.

**Question:** With rapid advances in information technology, companies can report their earnings on a daily basis or even by the minute. What value can be attached to all these earnings studies with continuous information?

**Dreman:** The cognitive psychologists talk about informational overload. When do we have enough information? They have measured—using handicaps in horse racing, for example—the relationships among accuracy, amount of information, and confidence. They have found that a certain number of informational inputs—say, 5—will generate a certain degree of accuracy; then they can measure the predictors' confidence. They increase the number of informational inputs—say, to 50—and they find that confidence goes way up but accuracy stays exactly the same.

Something similar may be going on in the investment industry with the availability of numerous and instantaneous data and information on analysts' changing expectations through such media as First Call. Figure 1 showed that analysts' estimates are getting worse with time. So, you might speculate that more information coming in at a faster rate results in greater analyst overconfidence.

**Question:** Russell Fuller's proposition was that large, predictable earnings are the route to good performance.[1] Are you suggesting that earnings surprise—maybe more accurately "low predictability"—is a better route to good performance?

**Dreman:** I do not disagree with what Fuller says. Our studies simply point out that predictability is very difficult and the probability of accurate predictions is low. The views are not in conflict; we simply have different investment approaches to the same problem. I feel more comfortable with translating the facts into a contrarian strategy, and Fuller probably feels more confident of his way.

[1] See Mr. Fuller's presentation, pp. 31–34.

# The Future of Behavioral Finance: A Synthesis of Disciplines

Horace "Woody" Brock
*President*
*Strategic Economic Decisions, Inc.*

Proponents of behavioral finance point out that real-world data do not fit the efficient markets paradigm very well. The proponents do so, however, by assuming that investors are irrational and biased. But to define someone as irrational is to presuppose the existence of a standard or a benchmark of rationality. This presentation describes a new approach in which the real-world behavior of asset prices is not the result of investor irrationality but of systematic mistakes investors make in their forecasts because of ignorance of the true structure of the economy.

My charge for this presentation is to sketch a synthesis of the contending approaches discussed in the seminar. I am going to do so partly by criticizing some of what we have heard and partly by proposing an alternative paradigm of how markets work. This new paradigm is emerging from research at Stanford University and was cited in the April 3, 1995, edition of *Fortune* in a story titled "Yes, You Can Beat the Market."

The efficient markets, capital asset pricing model paradigm has dominated thinking in financial economics for three decades. An industry of consultants grew up around it because the theory is simple and largely quantifiable. The mathematics are linear, which made the theory tractable. Nonetheless, proponents of behavioral finance have done a good job of embarrassing classical asset pricing theory by pointing out that real-world data do not fit the efficient market paradigm very well. In doing so, they place considerable emphasis on ways in which investors exhibit "biases" and are "irrational."

## Problems with Behavioral Finance

Having said that, I have three broad problems with the approach of behavioral finance. My first concern centers not on the issue of individual psychology and biases, but rather on how markets actually work given whatever biases may or may not exist. Knowing lots about the biases of the people making investment decisions tells us little about what results in the market, namely, the sequence of observed prices and quantities. What my clients want to know is how we can link up agents' beliefs (biased or not) with what markets are going to do in processing those beliefs. In this regard, the important thing to realize is that the connector between the input and the output—the invisible hand, the law of the market—is a highly complex, nonlinear operator. Its nature can be seen both theoretically and empirically in the fact that slight changes in the distribution of beliefs can cause vast changes in price and quantity outputs. Black Monday offers one example, and so does the bond market of 1994. If all that mattered were how biased agents are, then linearity or continuity would hold, but we know that it does not.

A second and much deeper problem with behavioral finance is that people are considered irrational because they allegedly exhibit certain kinds of biases. But to define someone as irrational in this manner is to presuppose some standard as a benchmark: An objective truth exists, and people are biased because they do not acknowledge this truth. The statement that someone is biased has no meaning without the prior assertion of a truth. But suppose people are wrong because they do not know, indeed cannot know, the true underlying structure of the economy because of structural changes, which in turn, cause the economy to be nonstationary. Then, the assertion that people are irrational has no meaning because the very meaning of "truth" in a nonstationary, stochastic system is ambiguous.

Finally, the putative irrationality from which we all allegedly suffer has a normative aspect. If the statement that most people have biases is true, then if I decide to hire you to invest my money, I do not want you managing my money with the kind of biases, contradictions, and irrationalities to which behavioral finance alludes. Rather, I want you to act rationally on my behalf and maximize my utility. Such conduct is known as "contingently normative behavior." In a principal–agent context, this point is very important. I should not pay a trustee to act irrationally—regardless of whether everyone else acts irrationally—because acting irrationally means, by definition, acting so as to contradict what I want to achieve.

## The Stanford Paradigm of Market Behavior

A very important point in the philosophy of science is that progress consists of replacing an old theory by generalizing it, not by throwing it out. Take, for example, what happened with game theory. Classical game theory as postulated by John von Neuman assumed that when we play a game, each of us knows the game. We know the rules of the game. I know your payoffs, and you know mine. In particular, I know your utility function, and you know mine. Under these strong assumptions, game theory did not live up to early hopes that it would explain and predict individual behavior. John Harsanyi, the 1994 Nobel laureate, did not throw out classical theory, however; rather, he generalized it by relaxing the assumption of complete information—that is, the assumption that each player knows the other's utility function. Once this was done, game theory could, in fact, explain all sorts of seemingly irrational phenomena. A new definition of "rationality" resulted.

A similar reconceptualization of the efficient market hypothesis within general equilibrium theory is currently being undertaken by Mordecai Kurz at Stanford University. This new paradigm allows us to explain how markets work in reality without assuming that people are dumb or irrational. Unlike behavioral finance, which throws the baby out with the bath water, the new paradigm extends the classical general equilibrium model in a way that permits explanation of such phenomena as excess performance (i.e., beating the market), excess volatility, trend-following behavior, and Black Monday, and it does so without having to assume any irrationality on the part of investors.

Central to this new paradigm is the reality that investors do not have and cannot have those unbiased forecasts, or rational expectations, found in textbooks. The rational expectations of the old theory are replaced in the new theory by the concept of rational beliefs. In the new paradigm, there is no need to introduce the assumption that investors are in some sense "irrational," even if the behavior of prices appears irrational. Investors may be irrational, as behavioral finance adherents believe, but no such assumption is *required* to generate the kind of real-world market data that, paradoxically, gave rise to behavioral finance in the first place. In the new approach, the behavior of asset prices is not the result of investor irrationality per se but, rather, of systematic mistakes investors make in their forecasts because of an ineluctable ignorance of the true structure of the economy.

The notion of making a forecast mistake is different from the notion of making a forecast error. Whereas there is no way in which to avoid making a forecast error other than by being lucky, one can indeed avoid making a forecast mistake, and (happily for "active" managers) can do so without relying solely on luck. Note, in this regard, that there are three ways to outperform the market: be lucky, obtain inside information, or gain an "inferential advantage" by interpreting common data better than others do. In the new paradigm, people can gain an inferential advantage and reduce systematic forecast mistakes by understanding structural changes better than and/or sooner than others do. The intelligent investor can now be ahead of the pack and make a smaller mistake than others. In other words, the investor will have been "right for the right reason." This—competing bets on the nature of structural change—is, in my view, what active investment management ought to be about.

## Classical Economics versus New Economics

Classical theory postulates a fixed, known (or "stationary") economic environment in which there are no interesting surprises. This fixed environment is one in which somebody with lots of data, using the law of large numbers, can find the truth. We all learn inductively the probability of $x$ given $y$; everyone knows it. It is unique, and everyone thus has the same forecast. This is called stationarity. Our forecasts are correct; market prices are efficient, and they embody the truth. Volatility is strictly proportional to shocks or news about fundamentals. Black Monday or price overshoot or trends in prices cannot occur because prices move in strict accord with "news," and returns constitute a random walk.

The new approach is replacing the classical approach by saying that the world is not stationary. Structural changes are the source of nonstationarity. The end of communism, the rise of OPEC (and the fall of OPEC), the advent of the microchip—all these things change functional relationships. So, the models have to be updated and refitted. Because investors cannot and do not know the true dynamic laws of the system, there is "model uncertainty." We do not know the true models. Therefore, we make forecast mistakes. And market prices are inefficient, in the sense that they reflect the aggregate mistakes of all investors.

Thus, a new variable is introduced into the foundations of the law of Adam Smith, or the law of the market, and it is called "the distribution of mistakes." This is Kurz's fundamental contribution. How many people are how wrong and how that distribution, that cluster of mistakes, changes over time are the fundamental grist that drives markets and causes them not to do what they would do in the textbook. All markets misprice everything because, as a result of structural change, the truth cannot be known.

Markets are inefficient, not because people are dumb (they are not), not because markets are sticky or corrupt (they are not), but because the vector of market-clearing prices in a world where we do not know the truth will clearly not be the vector that would be solved for if we all did know the truth. In real-world asset markets, people do not know the true pricing model any more than they know the truth about the structural relationships in the underlying economy (the true nature of the business cycle, the correct inflation–growth trade-off, and so on). Indeed, they cannot know the true pricing model because in a nonstationary world characterized by structural change, the true model is unlearnable from the data. This is a theorem, not an opinion.

This observation carries a profound implication: Because investors acknowledge that they do not have a completely reliable model with which to interpret the news correctly, it will be rational for them in certain cases to condition their forecasts of the future, in part, on the sequence of past prices. In the absence of knowledge of the true model, the path of past prices can reveal information useful to them in forecasting the future. In particular, past prices can reveal what others (e.g., the market as a whole) *believed* the true pricing model to have been.

In such a world, the resulting sequence of prices generated by market trading is much more chaotic than the sequence generated in the classical world. This excess-volatility problem, documented in the empirical results of Robert Shiller and others (see, for example, Shiller 1981), has been the great embarrassment to the efficient markets hypothesis. In the new paradigm, there will be periods when prices exhibit little or no trend and other periods when strong trends are clear. Under the old paradigm, this trend-following behavior would not be possible because the theory requires the assumption of rational expectations, meaning that we all know the truth up to a white-noise factor. (White noise represents uncertainty that cannot be reduced by learning; it is irrelevant.) That is, if everyone knows the true model perfectly, then the news is always perfectly priced and the path of past prices can tell nothing about the future. There will thus be no trend-following behavior in classical finance.

Strategic Economic Decisions conducted a study at the end of last summer on the 1994 European bond market and the 214 basis point rise in interest rates from January to June. That situation is an example of where the best and the brightest got it all wrong, and it is certainly not unique. We took a survey of 60 market makers (many of whom were people who caused the crash to happen) to discover their perceptions of what happened. As **Figure 1** shows, according to these market makers, 34 percent of the change in interest rates (73 basis points) was associated with news about inflation and 21 percent (45 bps), with market correction; the rest (96 bps) was attributed to the trinity of irrationality, inefficiency, and illiquidity.

**Figure 1. Reasons Given for the Rise in Rates in the January 1–June 21, 1994, European Bond Market**

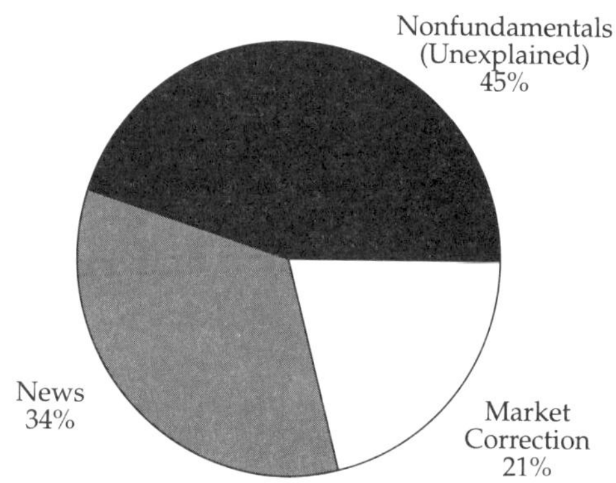


*Source*: Strategic Economic Decisions interviews.

In the world of classical economics, everything must be driven by news alone. The new theory not only permits but explains from first principles why you might observe the "market correction" and "unexplained" components of total volatility. The new theory would call the upper portion of the pie "endogenous uncertainty." Endogenous means that this unexplainable volatility is the result bubbling up from within the system of how many people are how wrong. More formally, the distribution of mistakes and how it intersects with the distribution of leverage is one key to effecting market overshoots, which makes sense: If everyone is wrong and the ones who are wrong are also the ones who are very leveraged, the result is a stampede for the exit. This is one point of the new paradigm: Market overshoots are not a result of irrationality per se but of systematic mistakes people may make in their forecasts because they do not know the true asset-pricing model. When mistakes are "clustered" and agents leveraged, all hell breaks loose.

The concept of model misbehavior—that is, the way prices bungee-jump the news in a way they are not supposed to—can be formalized in a measure I have introduced and called "omega risk." Omega risk is a measure of intrinsic volatility, or the degree of model uncertainty. It is the degree to which we do not understand the asset-pricing models with which we price the news. **Figure 2** shows the spectrum of omega risk for three asset classes—bonds, stocks, and currencies. In the case of T-bills and T-bonds, very simple, linear, one-equation, one-variable models are available that will let someone know roughly what will happen to bond prices if given an inflation shock. For these simple, reliable pricing models, omega risk is low. On the other hand, when uncertainty about the "true" underlying pricing model is high, as in the case of currencies, where no reliable pricing model exists, omega risk is high.

**Figure 2. Spectrum of Intrinsic Volatility: Omega Risk**

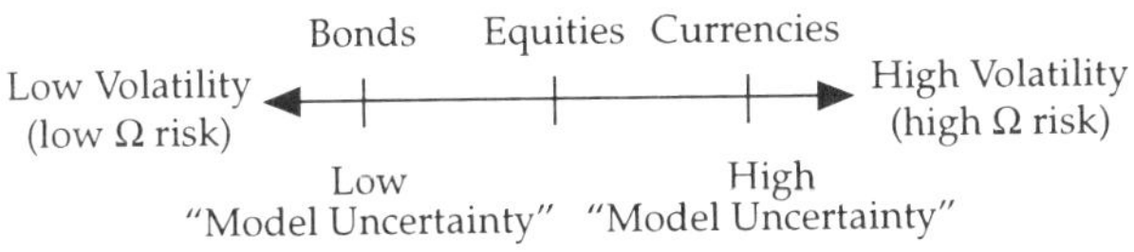


*Source*: Strategic Economic Decisions.

Formally, omega risk can be defined as actual variance divided by theoretical variance. Take a sample period *S*. In this period, we had news. It is past, so we can run the news through the bond market pricing model from classical theory and find at each point in time what the price should have been. From that information, we can figure out what the theoretical volatility should have been given the particular flow of news during period *S*. This theoretical variance of price is in the denominator, and the actual variance of prices observed in the period *S* goes in the numerator:

$$\Omega = \frac{\text{Actual variance}^{S}}{\text{Theoretical variance}^{S}}\ .$$

According to the new paradigm, the sequence of asset prices over time will sometimes exhibit an identifiable price trend that can probably be exploited by traders. These "trend regimes," or trend-following behavior, are characterized by a high degree of model uncertainty and high price overshoot; thus, values of omega for the regimes are greater than 1. At other times, the sequence of prices over time will not offer any exploitable price trends; "drift regimes" result, for which omega is less than 1.

**Figure 3** formalizes this concept at an abstract level in what is called the "wishbone" diagram. The

**Figure 3. The Wishbone Diagram**

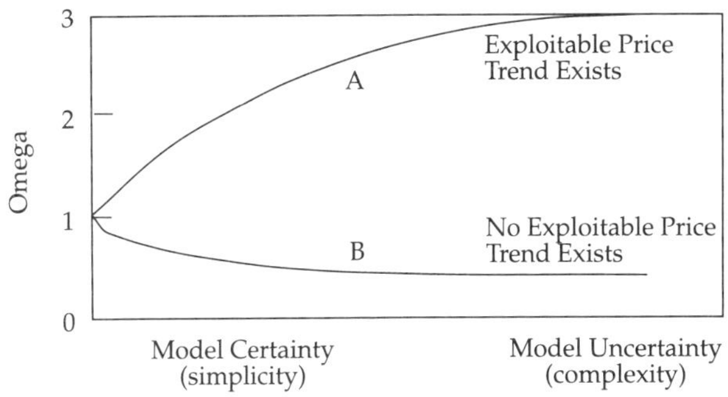


*Source*: Strategic Economic Decisions.

essential idea is that the magnitude of omega risk (both price overshooting and price undershooting) at a given time is a function of two different properties of a market: (1) whether or not an exploitable trend is revealed by recent price data and (2) the degree to which market participants do not understand or else do not believe in the underlying model in terms of which they should, ideally, "price" the news. At the far left of the horizontal axis is complete model certainty. In this case, traders and investors fully understand and act upon the pricing model; it is the domain of rational expectations economics. Here, the actual price will always be the same as the theoretical price forecast by the model. Actual volatility in such a regime will thus be the same as the theoretical volatility implied by the pricing model; omega will be equal to 1, as indicated by the left-hand cusp of the wishbone. There is no overshoot or undershoot of the news.

Now, move way out to the right of the spectrum to where model uncertainty is great, as would be the case with currencies, and consider a point in time when a price trend is discernible. Given high levels of model uncertainty, many people will decide to surf that trend, and precisely for that reason, prices will rise/fall much more than they would under the true model, causing omega to assume a value greater than 1. Moving back to the left on the same arc to a lesser level of model uncertainty (the case of bonds), trend-following behavior will be less pronounced because a good number of investors will retain a measure of belief in the true pricing model. Omega risk will clearly be less, which is why the upper arc of the wishbone rises: The greater the underlying model uncertainty, the greater the overshoot and, hence, the higher the values of omega.

An analogous, if obverse, logic governs the lower arc, which characterizes what happens as model uncertainty increases in the absence of any price trend. The greater the model uncertainty, the more people will become agnostic, likely to sit on the sidelines and ignore the news. Fractional values of omega result because actual volatility ends up much lower than the correct volatility implied by the true pricing model.

The arcs thus classify the two generic types of price regimes that we should (and do) observe in reality, especially in currencies. For example, I have long been interested in the notion of why bond pricing sort of makes sense while stock pricing makes less sense and currency movements are senseless. I wanted an axiomatic derivation from first principles of why this is true, and now we have it. Because omega levels are closer to unity for bonds, most of the time, the situation is less chaotic for bonds than for stocks and much less chaotic than for currencies.

## Conclusion

I am very much in accord with the views of people in behavioral finance; after all, how can one disagree with the notion that we are biased. But the problem is much deeper than bias. The problem is the fact that we cannot know the true structure of economic reality, and hence of price movements, because of model uncertainty and nonstationarity in the economic environment. Consequently, we are always wrong in varying degrees. This is not irrationality. Each of us, knowing that it is a nonstationary world, has a requirement to develop our own theory of how the world has changed.

I have outlined a new paradigm that is producing very exciting results about how markets work without postulating that people are dumb, biased, or irrational. The main point of this presentation is that although markets act strangely and people may be ignorant and biased, we should not discard the laws of the Adam Smith–Arrow–Debreu general equilibrium model of excess demand, excess supply, price adjustments, and so on. They are the guts of our life, of capitalism, of business, of markets. Unlike the theories postulated in behavioral finance, the new paradigm allows us to provide an alternative explanation of the behavior of real markets within a general equilibrium framework, but a framework general enough to encompass the existence and critical role of mistakes.

# Question and Answer Session

Horace "Woody" Brock

**Question:** If rational beliefs can predict Black Mondays, will we be able to use this theory to predict the next one, to make money?

**Brock:** What this new theory does is show that once you allow for the fact that people cannot know the truth and are wrong, the mathematics will turn out a sequence of prices and quantities. It does not predict the date a Black Monday is going to recur unless you know how to feed all the conditions (that is, the sequences of distributions of beliefs) of the original Black Monday into it. I do not think that will ever be possible. So, in that sense, the model isn't going to suddenly make you rich.

**Question:** How can investment managers exploit structural change? Can you give us some examples of changes managers could exploit?

**Brock:** The way you make money when you don't have private information is to know the structural change ahead of other people. If you do, then by definition, you will be less surprised by the news tomorrow than they will and you will make money at their expense. It is not enough to know the structural change, however; you also need to know when the rest of the market will catch on. The point Werner De Bondt made was quite correct: It takes time for people and markets to learn.[1] They were late figuring out the power of the OPEC cartel, and they were late realizing that it had to collapse.

A good current example of using your understanding before other people involves the fact that current inflation is lower than it "ought" to be with a 2.7 percent GDP growth rate. The true wealth of the economy last year, if you correct for the mismeasurement of inflation, grew at 5.5 percent, and the true inflation rate was about 1.3 percent.

These numbers are mind-bogglingly good, and people who understood them are making money. The people who will wait until 1998, because they need another 48 quarters to do their regressions, will lose. You have to take a risk. There is no costless way to get rich. This time around, the risk is that my inferences about structural change are better than yours, but because you cannot know whether this is true, it is not arbitrage. You have to *believe* that you are seeing things differently from the way the others are.

**Question:** How will you test the validity of your new axiomatic theory?

**Brock:** Testing this new theory is an ongoing process that will take 10–20 years probably, because like relativity theory, the material is difficult. Two major econometric studies have been done so far. Using stock market data from 1947 to 1992, previous theories on estimating volatility found an $R^2$ of about 0.32, whereas in tests with this theory—focusing on the facts that structural changes occur and people are wrong about them and late in learning them—the $R^2$ went to 0.72.

Let me give two examples. In about late 1966, the DJIA hit 1000. Why did it hit 1000? Investors were operating under the old regime, extrapolating the success of General Motors, the American post-World War II productivity gains, but they failed to realize that, in fact, we now had a decade of club management. The market, just as it did with the OPEC crisis, stalled and never recovered for 15 years. The same thing is going on today. I think the DJIA is at 4000 not because of a bubble but because of earnings surprise. (Earnings surprise cannot happen in classical economic theory.) Companies and the people who analyze the companies assumed that profits would be $\pi^*$ by assuming that costs would be a certain $C^*$. Because of structural changes in the cost function, however, costs have been much lower than expected; therefore, profits have been bigger than expected.

Both market lows and market highs can be shown to be the result of people being slow to recognize some structural change. If God had told everybody about the new OPEC regime and everyone had recognized it at once, you would have been right in the textbook world of the capital asset pricing model. The crucial point is nonstationarity, and it is not learnable enough in advance that everybody will recognize it, which produces the mistakes.

[1] See Mr. De Bondt's presentation, pp. 7–12.

# Bibliography


Abarbanell, Jeffrey S., and Victor Bernard. 1992. "Tests of Analysts' Overreaction/Underreaction to Earnings Information as an Explanation for Anomalous Stock Price Behavior." *The Journal of Finance* (July):1181–206.

Ali, Ashiq, April Klein, and James Rosenfeld. 1992. "Analysts' Use of Information about Permanent and Transitory Earnings Components in Forecasting Annual EPS." *The Accounting Review* (January):183–98.

Atkinson, Thomas R. 1967. *Trends in Corporate Bond Quality.* New York: Columbia University Press for the National Bureau of Economic Research.

Basi, Bart A., Kenneth J. Carey, and Richard D. Twark. 1976. "A Comparison of the Accuracy of Corporate and Security Analysts' Forecasts of Earnings." *The Accounting Review* (April):244–54.

Basu, Sanjoy. 1977. "Investment Performance of Common Stocks in Relation to Their Price–Earnings Ratios: A Test of the Efficient Markets Hypothesis." *The Journal of Finance* (June):663–82.

———. 1983. "The Relationship between Earnings' Yield, Market Value and Return for NYSE Common Stocks: Further Evidence." *Journal of Financial Economics* (June):129–56.

Bauman, W. Scott, and Richard Dowen. 1991. "Security Analyst Forecasts and the Earnings Yield Anomaly." Working paper, Northern Illinois University (December).

Benesh, Gary A., and Pamela P. Peterson. 1986. "On the Relation between Earnings Changes, Analysts' Forecasts and Stock Price Fluctuations." *Financial Analysts Journal* (November/December):29–39, 55.

Bernard, Victor L. 1993. "Stock Price Reactions to Earnings Announcements." In *Advances in Behavioral Finance*, R.H. Thaler (ed.). New York: Russell Sage Foundation.

Bernard, Victor L., and Jacob Thomas. 1989. "Post-Earnings-Announcement Drift: Delayed Price Response or Risk Premium?" *Journal of Accounting Research*, vol. 27 supplement:1–48.

Black, Fischer. 1976. "The Dividend Puzzle." *The Journal of Portfolio Management* (Winter):5–8.

Brealey, Richard A. 1968. *An Introduction to Risk and Return from Common Stocks.* Cambridge, MA: MIT Press.

Brown, Keith C., and W.V. Harlow. 1988. "Market Overreaction: Magnitude and Intensity." *The Journal of Portfolio Management* (Winter):6–13.

Brown, Lawrence D. 1993. "Earnings Forecasting Research: Its Implications for Capital Markets Research." *International Journal of Forecasting* (December).

Chopra, Navin, Josef Lakonishok, and Jay R. Ritter. 1992. "Measuring Abnormal Performance: Do Stocks Overreact?" *Journal of Financial Economics*, vol. 31, no. 2:235–68.

Cialdini, Robert B. 1984. *Influence: The Psychology of Persuasion.* New York: Quill, William Morrow.

Clark, John Maurice. 1918. "Economics and Modern Psychology." *Journal of Political Economy* (January).

Clarke, Roger, and Meir Statman. 1994. "Growth, Value, Good and Bad." *Financial Analysts Journal* (November/December):82–86.

Conrad, Jennifer, and Gautam Kaul. 1993. "Long-Term Overreaction or Biases in Computed Returns?" *The Journal of Finance* (March):39–63.

Constantinides, George M. 1983. "Capital Market Equilibrium with Personal Tax." *Econometrica* (May).

———. 1984. "Optimal Stock Trading with Personal Taxes: Implications for Prices and the Abnormal January Returns." *Journal of Financial Economics* (March):65–89.

Copeland, Ronald M., and Robert J. Marioni. 1972. "Executives' Forecasts of Earnings per Share versus Forecasts of Naive Models." *The Journal of Business* (October):497–512.

Cragg, John G., and Burton G. Malkiel. 1968. "The Consensus and Accuracy of Some Predictors of the Growth of Corporate Earnings." *The Journal of Finance* (March):67–84.

De Bondt, Werner F.M. 1991. "What Do Economists Know about the Stock Market?" *The Journal of Portfolio Management* (Winter):84–91.

———. 1992. *Earnings Forecasts and Share Price Reversals.* Charlottesville, VA: The Research Foundation of the Institute of Chartered Financial Analysts.

———. 1993. "Betting on Trends: Intuitive Forecasts of Financial Risk and Return." *International Journal of Forecasting* (December).

De Bondt, Werner F.M., and Richard H. Thaler. 1985. "Does the Stock Market Overreact?" *The Journal of Finance* (July):793–805.

———. 1987. "Further Evidence on Investor Overreaction and Stock Market Seasonality." *The Journal of Finance*, vol. 42, no. 3:557–80.

———. 1990. "Do Security Analysts Overreact?" *American Economic Review* (May):52–57.

———. Forthcoming. "Financial Decision-Making in Markets and Firms: A Behavioral Perspective." In *Handbook of Finance*, R. Jarrow et al. (eds.). Amsterdam, The Netherlands: Elsevier Science B.V.

Dowen, Richard J., and W. Scott Bauman. 1991. "Revisions in Corporate Earnings Forecasts and Common Stock Returns." *Financial Analysts Journal* (March/April):86–90.

Dreman, David N. 1977. *Psychology and the Stock Market: Investment Strategy beyond Random Walk.* New York: Amacom.

———. 1979. *The Contrarian Investment Strategy.* New York: Random House.

———. 1982. *The New Contrarian Investment Strategy.* New York: Random House.

Dreman, David N., and Michael A. Berry. 1995a. "Analyst Forecasting Errors and Their Implications for Security Analysts." *Financial Analysts Journal* (May/June):30–41.

———. 1995b. "Overreaction, Underreaction, and the Low-P/E Effect." *Financial Analysts Journal* (July/August):21–30.

Fama, Eugene F., and Kenneth R. French. 1992. "The Cross-Section of Expected Stock Returns." *The Journal of Finance* (June).

Fischhoff, B. 1982. "Debiasing." In *Judgment under Uncertainty: Heuristics and Biases*, D. Kahneman, P. Slovic, and A. Tversky (eds.). New York: Cambridge University Press.

Frisch, Deborah, and Robert T. Clemen. Forthcoming. "Beyond Expected Utility: Rethinking Behavioral Decision Research." *Psychological Bulletin*.

Fuller, Russell, Lex C. Huberts, and Michael J. Levinson. 1993. "Returns to E/P Strategies, Higgledy-Piggledy Growth, Analysts' Forecast Errors, and Omitted Risk Factors." *The Journal of Portfolio Management* (Winter):13–24.

Graham, Benjamin, and David Dodd. 1962. *Security Analysis: Principles and Techniques*, 3rd ed. New York: McGraw-Hill.

Green, David, and Joel Segal. 1967. "The Predictive Power of First Quarter Earnings Reports." *The Journal of Business* (January):44–55.

Grinold, Richard, and Andrew Rudd. 1987. "Incentive Fees: Who Wins? Who Loses?" *Financial Analysts Journal* (January/February):27–38.

Gross, LeRoy. 1982. *The Art of Selling Intangibles: How to Make Your Million($) by Investing Other People's Money*. New York: New York Institute of Finance.

Harlow, W.V., and Keith C. Brown. 1990. *The Role of Risk Tolerance in the Asset Allocation Process: A New Perspective*. Charlottesville, VA: The Research Foundation of the Institute of Chartered Financial Analysts.

Hickman, W. Braddock. 1958. *Corporate Bond Quality and Investor Experience*. New Jersey: Princeton University Press for the National Bureau of Economic Research.

Hogarth, Robin M., and Melvin W. Reder (eds.). 1986. *Rational Choice*. Chicago, IL: University of Chicago Press.

Huberts, Lex C., and Russell J. Fuller. 1995. "Predictability Bias in the U.S. Equity Market." *Financial Analysts Journal* (March/April):12–28.

Imhoff, Eugene A., and Paul V. Pare. 1982. "Analysis and Comparison of Earnings Forecast Agents." *Journal of Accounting Research* (Autumn):429–39.

Kahneman, Daniel, and Amos Tversky. 1972. "Subjective Probability: A Judgment of Representativeness." *Cognitive Psychology* (July):430–54.

_____. 1979. "Prospect Theory: An Analysis of Decision Making under Risk." *Econometrica*:263-91.

_____. 1982. "The Psychology of Preferences." *Scientific American* (January–June):167–73.

_____. 1984. "Choices, Values, and Frames." *American Psychologist*, vol. 39:341–50.

Kahneman, Daniel, Paul Slovic, and Amos Tversky (eds.). 1982. *Judgment under Uncertainty: Heuristics and Biases*. New York: Cambridge University Press.

Klein, April, and James Rosenfeld. 1991. "PE Ratios, Earnings Expectations, and Abnormal Returns." *Journal of Financial Research* (Spring):51–64.

Kothari, S.P., Jay Shenken, and Richard G. Sloan. 1995. "Another Look at the Cross-Section of Expected Stock Returns." *The Journal of Finance* (March).

Lakonishok, Josef, Andrei Shleifer, and Robert W. Vishny. 1992. "The Structure and Performance of the Money Management Industry." *Brookings Papers in Microeconomics*. Washington, DC: The Brookings Institute.

_____. 1994. "Contrarian Investment, Extrapolations, and Risk." *The Journal of Finance* (December):1541–78.

Latane, H., C. Jones, and R.D. Rieke. 1974. "Quarterly Earnings Reports and Subsequent Holding Period Returns." *Journal of Business Research* (April).

Little, I.M.D., and A.C. Rayner. 1966. *Higgledy-Piggledy Growth Again*. Oxford, England: Basil Blackwell.

Loughran, Tim, and Jay R. Ritter. 1995. "The New Issues Puzzle." *The Journal of Finance* (March):23–51.

McDonald, C.L. 1973. "An Empirical Examination of the Reliability of Published Predictions of Future Earnings." *The Accounting Review*, vol. 48:502.

McDonald, John G., and Donald C. Baron. 1973. "Risk and Return on Short Positions in Common Stocks." *The Journal of Finance* (March):97–107.

Merton, Robert C., Myron S. Scholes, and Matthew L. Gladstein. 1978. "The Returns and Risk of Alternative Call Option Portfolio Investment Strategies." *The Journal of Business*, vol. 51, no. 2:183–242.

Michaely, R., R. Thaler, and K. Womack. 1994. "Price Reactions to Dividend Initiations and Omissions: Overreaction or Drift?" Working paper, Cornell University.

Miller, Merton H. 1986. "Behavioral Rationality in Finance: The Case of Dividends." *Journal of Business* 4:S451–68.

Miller, Merton H., and F. Modigliani. 1961. "Dividend Policy, Growth, and the Valuation of Shares." *The Journal of Business* (October):411–33.

Neiderhoffer, Victor, and Patrick J. Regan. 1972. "Earnings Changes, Analysts' Forecasts and Stock Prices." *Financial Analysts Journal* (May/June):65–71.

Nicholson, Francis. 1968. "Price–Earnings Ratios." *Financial Analysts Journal* (January/February):105–9.

Ou, Jane A., and Stephen H, Penman. 1989. "Accounting Measurement, Price–Earnings Ratio, and the Information Content of Security Prices." *Journal of Accounting Research*, vol. 27 supplement:111–52.

Paulos, John Allen. 1988. *Innumeracy*. New York: Hill and Wang.

Poundstone, William. 1992. *Prisoner's Dilemma*. New York: Anchor Books.

Record, Eugene E., Jr., and Mary Ann Tynan. 1987. "Incentive Fees: The Basic Issues." *Financial Analysts Journal* (January/February):39–43.

Reinganum, Marc R. 1981. "Misspecification of Capital Asset Pricing: Empirical Anomalies Based on Earnings Yields and Market Values." *Journal of Financial Economics*, vol. 9, no. 1:19–46.

Rendleman, Richard J., Charles P. Jones, and Henry A. Latane. 1982. "Empirical Anomalies Based on Unexpected Earnings and the Importance of Risk Adjustments." *Journal of Financial Economics*, vol. 10, no. 3:269–87.

———. 1987. "Further Insight into the Standardized Unexpected Earnings Anomaly: Size and Serial Correlation Effects." *The Financial Review* (February):131–44.

Richards, R. Malcolm. 1976. "Analysts' Performance and the Accuracy of Corporate Earnings Forecasts." *The Journal of Business* (July):350–57.

Richards, R. Malcolm, and Donald R. Fraser. 1977. "Further Evidence of the Accuracy of Analysts' Earnings Forecasts: A Comparison among Analysts." *Journal of Economics and Business* (Spring/Summer):244–54.

Richards, R. Malcolm, James J. Benjamin, and Robert W. Strawser. 1977. "An Examination of the Accuracy of Earnings Forecasts." *Financial Management* (Fall):78–86.

Ritter, Jay. 1991. "The Long-Run Performance of Initial Public Offerings." *The Journal of Finance* (March):3–27.

Ross, Stephen A. 1989. "Institutional Markets, Financial Marketing, and Financial Innovation." *The Journal of Finance* (July):541–56.

Saunders, Edward, M., Jr. 1993. "Stock Prices and Wall Street Weather." *The American Economic Review* (December).

Shefrin, Hersh, and Meir Statman. 1984. "Explaining Investor Preference for Cash Dividends." *Journal of Financial Economics* (June):253–82.

———. 1985. "The Disposition to Sell Winners Too Early and Ride Losers Too Long: Theory and Evidence." *The Journal of Finance*, vol. 40, no. 3:777–82.

———. 1986. "How Not to Make Money in the Stock Market." *Psychology Today* (February).

———. 1992. *Ethics, Fairness, Efficiency, and Financial Markets*. Charlottesville, VA: The Research Foundation of the Institute of Chartered Financial Analysts.

———. 1993a. "Behavioral Aspects of the Design and Marketing of Financial Products." *Financial Management* (Summer).

———. 1993b. "Ethics, Fairness, and Efficiency in Financial Markets." *Financial Analysts Journal* (November/December):21–29.

———. 1995a. "Behavioral Portfolio Theory." Working paper, Santa Clara University.

———. 1995b. "Making Sense of Beta, Size, and Book-to-Market." *The Journal of Portfolio Management* (Winter).

———. 1995c. "Behavioral Capital Asset Pricing Theory." *Journal of Financial and Quantitative Analysis* (September).

Shiller, Robert J. 1981a. "Do Stock Prices Move Too Much to Be Justified by Subsequent Changes in Dividends?" *The American Economic Review* (June).

_____. 1981b. "The Use of Volatility Measures in Assessing Market Efficiency." *The Journal of Finance*, vol 36., no. 2:291-304.

Slovic, Paul. Forthcoming. "The Construction of Preference." *American Psychologist*.

Statman, Meir. 1988. "Investor Psychology and Market Inefficiencies." In *Equity Markets and Valuation Methods*, Katrina F. Sherrerd (ed.). Charlottesville, VA: The Institute of Chartered Financial Analysts.

———. 1995. "A Behavioral Framework for Dollar-Cost-Averaging." *The Journal of Portfolio Management* (Fall).

Statman, Meir, and D. Caldwell. 1987. "Applying Behavioral Finance to Capital Budgeting: Project Terminations." *Financial Management* (Winter):7–15.

Statman, Meir, Roger Clarke, and S. Krase. 1994. "Tracking Errors, Regret and Tactical Asset Allocation." *The Journal of Portfolio Management* (Spring).

Statman, Meir, and J. Sepe. 1989. "Project Termination Announcements and the Market Value of the Firm." *Financial Management* (Winter):74–81.

Statman, Meir, and M. Solt. 1988. "How Useful Is the Sentiment Index?" *Financial Analysts Journal* (September/October):45–55.

———. 1989. "Good Companies, Bad Stocks." *The Journal of Portfolio Management* (Summer):39–44.

Stewart, Samuel S., Jr. 1973. "Research Report on Corporate Forecasts." *Financial Analysts Journal* (January/February):77–85.

Stober, Thomas L. 1992. "Summary Financial Statement Measures and Analysts' Forecasts of Earnings." *Journal of Accounting and Economics*, vol. 15:347–72.

Thaler, Richard H. 1992. *The Winner's Curse*. New York: The Free Press.

Thaler, Richard H., and Hersh Shefrin. 1981. "The Economic Theory of Self-Control." *Journal of Political Economy* (April).

Tversky, Amos, and D. Kahneman. 1981. "The Framing of Decisions and the Psychology of Choice," AAAS.

———. 1986. "Rational Choice and the Framing of Decisions." *The Journal of Business* (October):S251–78.

von Neumann, John, and O. Morgenstern. 1944. *Theory of Games and Economic Behavior*. New Jersey: Princeton University Press.

Wiggins, James. 1991. "The Earnings–Price and Standardized Unexpected Earnings Effects: One Anomaly or Two?" *The Journal of Financial Research* (Fall):263–75.

Willis, Clint. 1990. "The Ten Mistakes to Avoid with Your Money." *Money* (June).

Zarowin, Paul. 1989. "Does the Stock Market Overreact to Corporate Earnings Information?" *The Journal of Finance* (December):1385–400.

———. 1990. "Size, Seasonality, and Stock Market Overreaction." *Journal of Financial and Quantitative Analysis* (March):113–26.

# Self-Evaluation Examination

1. In an empirical test of the correlation between value as a long-term investment and quality of management (according to *Fortune* survey respondents), Shefrin and Statman found:
   a. zero correlation.
   b. positive correlation.
   c. negative correlation.
   d. insignificant results.

2. In the same study, Statman and Shefrin also found a statistically significant relationship between value as a long-term investment and:
   a. beta.
   b. debt ratio.
   c. size.
   d. industry classification.

3. Which of the following behaviors violates the basic assumptions of the classical economic model of decision making:
   a. overconfidence.
   b. mental accounting.
   c. risk attitudes.
   d. all of the above.

4. According to De Bondt, actual prices are less volatile than prices using a well-calibrated dividend discount model.
   a. true.
   b. false.

5. De Bondt concludes that investors can benefit the most from insights into human behavior in:
   a. their long-run investment strategies.
   b. their short-run investment strategies.
   c. both long- and short-run investment strategies.
   d. neither long- nor short-run investment strategies.

6. Behavioral research on the effects of incentive fees provides evidence that they increase accuracy significantly by building confidence in judgments.
   a. true.
   b. false.

7. Research into behavioral decision making suggests that a good decision-making process has the following basic feature:
   a. it is based on an accurate assessment of the world.
   b. it is based on a consideration of relevant consequences.
   c. it includes trade-offs of some form.
   d. all of the above.

8. Research on the relationship between the predictability of earnings and investor returns shows that, *in relation to low-predictability stocks*:
   a. high-predictability stocks provide higher returns with less risk.
   b. high-predictability stocks provide higher returns with more risk.
   c. high-predictability stocks provide lower returns with less risk.
   d. high-predictability stocks provide lower returns with more risk.

9. Pzena argues that companies should pay analysts for their stock picks rather than for their earnings forecasts so that the research emphasis will be on good stocks rather than good companies.
   a. true.
   b. false.

10. In a study of analyst accuracy in forecasting earnings, Dreman and Berry found that analysts were able to hit within 10 percent of actual earnings:
    a. about 40 percent of the time.
    b. about 50 percent of the time.
    c. about 60 percent of the time.
    d. about 70 percent of the time.

11. According to behavioral research, for a company that is trading at a very low price-to-earnings, price-to-book, or price-to-cash-flow ratio and is believed to have a mediocre outlook, neither a negative nor a positive event is likely to have a major effect on the stock price.
    a. true.
    b. false.

12. Brock argues that the behavior of asset prices is the result of:
    a. investor rationality.
    b. investor irrationality.
    c. systematic mistakes investors make in their forecasts because of behavioral biases.
    d. systematic mistakes investors make in their forecasts because of ignorance of the true structure of the economy.

# Self-Examination Answers

1. b. They found a highly significant positive correlation, which suggests that people believe good stocks are the stocks of good companies. Statman notes that the opposite is true.

2. c. Statman and Shefrin found a statistically significant positive relationship between value as a long-term investment and size and a statistically significant negative relationship between value as a long-term investment and book value to market value.

3. d. Overconfidence, mental accounting, and risk attitudes are three areas of "cognitive illusion" that violate the basic assumptions of the classical economic model of decision making. See Tversky.

4. b. False. De Bondt shows that actual prices are more volatile than estimated prices.

5. d. De Bondt concludes that the insights about human behavior do not offer ways to make lots of money in the short run and that the payoff for long-run strategies is unclear. He suggests, however, that investors use contrarian strategies.

6. b. False. Shaw reports that incentives more often lead to the phenomenon of overconfidence in judgment and a deterioration in performance.

7. d. Shaw describes the reasoning behind these criteria.

8. a. Fuller suggests that the reason for this surprising result is that analysts seriously overestimate the next year's earnings for low-predictability companies.

9. b. False. Pzena states that, to defend against emotional decision making, firms should motivate analysts to focus on long-term earnings forecasts rather than current conditions in the stock market.

10. a. Dreman reports that 57 percent of analysts could not hit within 10 percent of actual; only 43 percent could.

11. b. False. Dreman reports that negative news for an out-of-favor stock has little effect on the stock price but positive news for such a company can have a very positive effect.

12. d. Brock argues that because we cannot know the true structure of economic reality and, hence, of price movements, we are wrong to varying degrees in our estimates of asset prices.

# Selected Publications*

## AIMR

**Managing Assets for Individual Investors,** 1995 . . . . . . . . . . . . . . . . . . . . . . . . . . $30
Sanjiv Bhatia, *Editor*

**Value and Growth Styles in Equity Investing,** 1995 . . . . . . . . . . . . . . . . . . . . . . . . $30
Jan R. Squires, CFA, *Editor*

**Corporate Financial Decision Making and Equity Analysis,** 1995 . . . . . . . . . . . . $30
Randall S. Billingsley, CFA, *Editor*

**Credit Analysis of Nontraditional Debt Securities,** 1995 . . . . . . . . . . . . . . . . . . . $30
Ashwinpaul C. Sondhi, *Editor*

**Performance Evaluation, Benchmarks, and Attribution Analysis,** 1995 . . . . . . . . $30
Jan R. Squires, CFA, *Editor*

**Real Estate Investing in the 1990s,** 1995 . . . . . . . . . . . . . . . . . . . . . . . . . . . . . $30
Susan Hudson-Wilson, *Editor*

**Fixed-Income Management: Techniques and Practices,** 1994 . . . . . . . . . . . . . . . $30
Dwight D. Churchill, CFA, *Editor*

**Blending Quantitative and Traditional Equity Analysis,** 1994 . . . . . . . . . . . . . . $30
H. Russell Fogler, *Editor*

**Investment Policy,** 1994 . . . . . . . . . . . . . . . . . . . . . . . . . . . . . . . . . . . . . . . . $30
Jan R. Squires, CFA, *Editor*

**Investing Worldwide V,** 1994 . . . . . . . . . . . . . . . . . . . . . . . . . . . . . . . . . . . . . $30

**The Automotive Industry,** 1994 . . . . . . . . . . . . . . . . . . . . . . . . . . . . . . . . . . . $30
Theodore Shasta, CFA, *Editor*

**The Telecommunications Industry,** 1994 . . . . . . . . . . . . . . . . . . . . . . . . . . . . . $30
Randall S. Billingsley, CFA, *Editor*

## Research Foundation

**Interest Rate and Currency Swaps: A Tutorial,** 1995 . . . . . . . . . . . . . . . . . . . . . $30
Keith C. Brown, CFA, and Donald J. Smith

**Bankruptcy Prediction Using Artificial Neural Systems,** 1995 . . . . . . . . . . . . . . $20
Robert E. Dorsey, Robert O. Edmister, and John D. Johnson

**Time Diversification Revisited,** 1995 . . . . . . . . . . . . . . . . . . . . . . . . . . . . . . . . $30
William Reichenstein, CFA, and Dovalee Dorsett

**Ethics in the Investment Profession: An International Survey,** 1995 . . . . . . . . . . . $20
H. Kent Baker, CFA, E. Theodore Veit, CFA, and Michael R. Murphy, CFA

**Corporate Governance and Firm Performance,** 1994 . . . . . . . . . . . . . . . . . . . . . . $20
Jonathan M. Karpoff, M. Wayne Marr, Jr., and Morris G. Danielson

**Analysts' Earnings Forecast Accuracy in Japan and the United States,** 1994 . . . . . $20
Robert M. Conroy, Robert S. Harris, and Young S. Park

*A full catalog of publications is available on AIMR's World Wide Web site: (http://www.aimr.com/aimr.html), or you may write to P.O. Box 3668, Charlottesville, VA 22903 U.S.A; call 1-804-980-3668; fax 1-804-980-9755; or e-mail (info@aimr.com) to receive a free copy. All prices are subject to change.

# AIMR PUBLICATIONS CATALOG ORDER FORM

PBD, Inc., P. O. Box 6996, Alpharetta, Georgia 30239-6996
(800) 789-AIMR or (404) 442-8633, ext. 266; fax (404) 442-9742; e-mail aimrpubs@pbd.com
(Effective December 1, 1995, the 404 area code will change to 770.)

**Shipping Information:**
UPS will not deliver to a post office box.

Name ______________________________

Company ______________________________

Street Address ______________________ Suite/Floor __________

City/Province ______________ State/Country ______________ ZIP/Postal Code __________

Daytime Telephone ______________ Fax ______________ E-mail __________

**Method of Payment:**
All orders must be prepaid by credit card, money order, or check.

☐ Check or money order enclosed (payable to PBD, Inc.)

☐ American Express ☐ VISA ☐ MasterCard ☐ Discover

___ ___ ___ ___ ___ ___ ___ ___ ___ ___ ___ ___ ___ ___ ___ ___

Signature ______________________ Expiration Date __________

| Item Code | Title | Quantity | Price Each | Total Price |
|---|---|---|---|---|
| | | | | |
| | | | | |
| | | | | |
| | | | | |
| | | | | |

**Canada Brokerage Fees**

| Dollar Value of Texts Ordered | | | Add to Order |
|---|---|---|---|
| US$ 0.01 | – | 40.00 | US$ 5.75 |
| US$ 40.01 | – | 100.00 | US$15.60 |
| US$ 100.01 | – | 200.00 | US$18.40 |
| US$ 200.01 | – | 350.00 | US$22.80 |
| US$ 350.01 | – | 500.00 | US$25.30 |
| US$ 500.01 | – | 750.00 | US$27.85 |
| US$ 750.01 | – | 1,000.00 | US$31.70 |
| US$1,000.01 | – | 1,250.00 | US$37.45 |
| US$1,250.01 | – | 1,500.00 | US$40.50 |
| US$1,500.01 | – | 5,000.00 | US$43.00 |

For each additional US$1,000 or fraction thereof, a charge of US$2.50 applies.

Total cost of books $__________

Discount (see below) –__________

Subtotal __________

Georgia residents add 6% sales tax __________

New York residents add 8.25% sales tax __________

Canadian residents add:
7% GST (#R123011536) __________
Brokerage fee (see table at left) __________

Shipping charges (see below)
☐ Priority or Air Freight __________

**Total cost of order** $__________

**Discounts:**
Professors, libraries, and orders of 50 or more copies of the same title qualify for a 25 percent discount. **NO DISCOUNTS APPLY TO MEMBER BOOK SERVICE BOOKS.**

**Shipping Methods:**

| | **Ground** | **Priority** |
|---|---|---|
| *U.S.* | No charge | $5.00 per order for the first book, plus $1.00 for each additional book (next day delivery). |
| | **Ground** | **Air Freight** |
| *Canada** | No charge | US$10.00 per order for the first book, plus US$2.00 for each additional book (1-3 day delivery). |
| *International* | Not available | US$10.00 per order for the first book, plus US$2.50 for each additional book (7-10 day delivery). |

*All Canadian orders must include brokerage fees and 7% GST.